P9-BZG-607

Loving *for a* Lifetime

6 *Essentials for a Happy, Healthy, and Holy Marriage*

RICHARD P. JOHNSON, PH.D.

Liguori
Lifespan

ONE LIGUORI DRIVE, LIGUORI, MO, 63057-9999

Thanks to Sister Matthias Haberberger, RSM, who assisted me with Bible citations and so much more.

Imprimi Potest:
Richard Thibodeau, C.Ss.R.
Provincial, Denver Province
The Redemptorists

ISBN 0-7648–0820-6
Library of Congress Catalog Card Number: 2001093202

© 2002, Richard P. Johnson, Ph.D.
Printed in the United States of America
06 05 04 03 02   5 4 3 2 1

Liguori Lifespan is an imprint of Liguori Publications.

All rights reserved. No part of this book may be reproduced, stored in a retrieval system, or transmitted without the written permission of Liguori Publications.

Scripture quotations are from the *New Revised Standard Version of the Bible*, copyright © 1989 by the Division of Christian Education of the National Council of Churches of Christ in the USA. Used with permission. All rights reserved.

To order, call 1-800-325-9521
www.liguori.org
www.catholicbooksonline.com

Table of Contents

To Sandra,
my loving marriage partner
for thirty-four years,
my spouse,
my life journey partner,
my best friend,
my salvation helper,
my earthly everything,
my only confidante,
my only love.

Introduction

H ave you ever wondered about the marvelous ingredients that must be in the "glue" that binds together long-lasting—"seasoned"—marriage relationships? These are the relationships that have grown for twenty-five or more years. Such relationships have prospered due to many factors, yet there must be some fundamental commonalities, some constant bedrock foundation qualities, that sustain and enliven such seasoned relationships, and give them the necessary internal fortitude to thrive across the span of a lifetime.

I've written this book from the perspectives of being a husband, a father of adult, married children, and a professional Christian counselor. I don't know whether I've learned more from my God-given role as a husband, my honored role as a father, or from my chosen profession as a counselor. Each has been a master teacher for me, and I have drawn upon each in writing this book. I've learned much about what makes for a happy, healthy, and holy marriage. I've learned experientially from the growing relationship my wife Sandy and I share, and I've learned vicariously from the hundreds of marriages that have sought relief in my counseling office.

This book is my attempt to synthesize what I've learned, and to organize it in some understandable framework so that you may find it useful in your own marital journey. What you'll find in these pages is my answer to what I believe marriages need most: seasoned insight into how to create, maintain, and, most of all, enjoy the beautiful marriage relationship we've been given.

I hope this doesn't seem like advice, which can sometimes seem haughty, superior, and/or moralistic. I offer you these pages in a spirit of respect of who you are, and in awe of what you are. I offer these words from my heart with reverence, gratitude, and in the hope that you may benefit even minimally from what I've been able to glean from my life so far.

As a Husband

Sandy and I have lived together in holy matrimony for more than thirty years. We've weathered a lot, and learned a lot. I have been blessed over these years with a partner whose distinctiveness and uniqueness I have still not fully fathomed—there remain points of mystery in and about her that I probably will never understand. I think this is good and healthy for our marriage. The mystery that is still part of her intrigues me, excites me, keeps me "on my toes," and blesses me with a depth of love I can never fully comprehend. There was a time in my life when I wanted to understand everything, and when I thought I actually could understand everything. I'm happy to report that time is long past. I now recline in the peace of God's mystery, knowing full well that Sandy is part of it.

Sandy is my model of the ideal spouse. As I wrote this book, my mental blueprint for a self-possessed, respectful, communicative, intimate, trusting, and committed spouse was always Sandy. She is my foundation, touchstone, keystone, and only love. I'm so pleased that Sandy is both my lover and best friend, and my only confidante. She's my steadfast and deep keel in the water of life. She steadies me, she tantalizes me, she impassions me, she makes me strong, and has the power to do almost anything to me. I trust her with my life. She would never intentionally hurt me. Over the years, there have been times when she has hurt me, or more accurately, when I've felt hurt. In hindsight, I realize that my hurt was my own doing. There have been many more times when I'm sure I hurt her. But again, I would never want to—or intentionally try to—hurt her.

As a Parent

I believe that every parent wants the very best for his or her children. I certainly do. However, as I review my "fatherly career" with my own children—the childhood years, adolescence, emerging adulthood, marriage, and advancing parenthood—I have a tendency to see more clearly what I should have done, the way I could have been, and how I should have acted toward them. In my own mind, the times I erred as a parent seem more starkly impressed on my mind than the times I didn't. Perhaps this is my own guilt at work, but I seem to remember thoughtlessly sharp words, times of self-absorbed indifference, and times when I mindlessly criticized them, more than I remember all the wonderful times that I know far outweigh the times when I wasn't at my best. For all those times, I'm truly sorry; I ask their forgiveness.

As a father, I still ask the same question that I have asked all along: What is it that my children need most from me at this time? Naturally, as they grew from one stage to another, their needs changed. Through it all, however, they always needed my love, blessing, nurturance, affirmation, example, and presence. Having journeyed with them over their life course to date, and having downshifted the level, intensity, duration, as well as the kind of support and guidance to match their changing needs as best I could, I now ask myself: What do they need most from me *now?* They no longer need me to teach them to walk, talk, read, or swing a baseball bat. They have stopped needing me to have a chat with their teacher, their coach, a neighbor, or even a police officer. They have even eclipsed their need for financial support from us. They have learned very well, and I now revel in their success.

What do they need the most from me now? My answer is that they need *me!* Not my physical presence, for some day we know that we'll be separated when God calls. What they need is my spiritual presence, which will live with them their whole lives. They need to know that I am thankful for their being exactly who they are, and that I love them more deeply every day.

As a Professional Counselor

As a professional counselor, I am privileged to be invited into the inner workings of many marriages. Some couples come to me for marriage counseling because of pain and "trouble" in the relationship. I see inside other relationships for very different reasons. Perhaps one spouse suffers from a depression, another experiences questions related to career direction. Child rearing is always a common concern, as is stress, bereavement, etc.

For twenty-five years, God has brought people to me. Most of them entered my counseling office carrying heavy emotional pain and personal need—some in psychological contortion, and many in spiritual turmoil. They are all good people who struggle in the holy light of God's illumination. I try very hard to see them in God's light; sometimes it's easier than others. There are few—if any—of these people of God who are not genuinely and intensely concerned about their families, and particularly about their marriages. Whatever the problem, issue, or concern that brings them into counseling, their marriage is always there as a backdrop, at the very least, and much more often as the centerpiece of their lives. When their marriages are life-giving, whole, and fulfilling, they can address and triumph over even the most challenging, wearisome, and seemingly insurmountable life problems. When their marriages are lifeless, fragmented, and dispirited, they seem powerless to get a grip on their lives in any healthy way.

This book is my small attempt to offer spouses (including our own children and their spouses) my simple gleanings on how to live a happy, healthy, and holy married life. My marriage to Sandy is the center of my life. I consider marriage the social centerpiece of our culture, the source of our earthly happiness, and the pathway to our vocation leading us to eternal life. There could be no more important endeavor than mastering the essentials of this sacred life we call marriage.

As you will see, marriage is a conundrum of opposites that constantly seek union, harmony, integration, and wholeness, all of which make us the people we are. Physical needs, mental well-being, social interaction needs, psychological functions, and spiritual growth needs all seek expression. Our job is to come to know ourselves as best we can, to help our spouse know him or herself as well as possible, and to work together to know God as best we can.

I offer you these ideas as an ongoing prayer of petition that you may open yourself fully to God, as a prayer of thanksgiving for all you've received, and as a prayer of praise to God for recognizing the power and the glory that flows from God alone.

Notes

CHAPTER ONE

Three Levels of Marital Interaction

As God's chosen ones, holy and beloved, clothe yourselves with compassion, kindness, humility, meekness, and patience. Bear with one another and, if anyone has a complaint against another, forgive each other; just as the Lord has forgiven you, so you also must forgive.

COLOSSIANS 3:12-13

E very marriage is a holy relationship, and no two relationships are alike—God has established in each marriage a unique gift and reflection of inexhaustible love. *All* the events in your marriage relationship offer lessons for life and for loving. The vocation of marriage is a lifelong course for learning how to love well. We can incorporate these lessons of loving into our own search for authenticity and salvation. As we make our way through life, we are continuously building our marriage in our own special ways, striving to make it so strong that the love we learn will last for a lifetime.

Relationships are not made with a cookie cutter; each is unlike any other. I believe that each marriage deserves its own book-length biography, since I have no doubt that such books are written on the hearts of all spouses who seek their ultimate salvation by living and working in the vocation of marriage.

Successfully seasoned and seasoning marriages[1] require skills, knowledge, and competencies on three levels:

1. The individual level—how each partner relates intrapersonally, to his or her own self.
2. The couple level—how each partner relates interpersonally to his or her spouse.
3. The spiritual level—how the couple relates to God.

Each of the next six chapters is divided into three sections which correspond to these three levels as its organizing framework.

1. The Individual Level: Expressing Your Unique Gifts

What we bring into our marriages, of course, is ourselves. We bring our distinctive personality, which contains the wonder of our God-given gifts that invest in each of us the magnificent reflection of God that makes us who we are. The most successful and fulfilling marriages—not to mention the most holy marriages—are the ones that have found ways for each spouse to freely and comfortably express his or her unique personality gifts. When you function in and from your gifts, you function at your best: you are most happy, productive, satisfied, healthy, and holy.

As a marriage partner, then, your fundamental goal is to help your spouse fully express his or her own distinct gifts. Unfortunately, this is never easy, especially in the early years of marriage when we are still building pathways of

---

[1] I use the descriptor "seasoned marriage" to describe a marriage that has found a continuing source of renewal, thereby creating happiness, healthfulness, and holiness over the long term. For our purposes, a marriage becomes "seasoned" when it has lasted twenty-five or more years. A "seasoning" marriage is one that is growing well, but has not yet made the twenty-five year mark.

communication. The couples who find their way to my counseling office have not found ways of expressing their own uniqueness, and have not succeeded in facilitating the expression of one another's gifts. On the contrary, these couples have either never discovered durable ways of helping to express the gifts of each other, or the relationship has degenerated into a pattern of interaction that suppresses rather than encourages the vital relationship building endeavor of freely expressing the unique gifts of each individual.

Your Six Premier Individual Gifts

While the reasons this blockage occurs are legion, the underlying theme of the blockage is always the same: individual baggage is getting in the way of the gift. In this volume, you'll explore the six premier individual gifts that give you the unique love-power necessary to find happiness in your marriage. You are called to use these six gifts every day of your married life. When given freedom of expression, these six gifts inspirit your relationship with the freshness and beauty of life and love. Your gifts have this power because your gifts are from God; they are gifts of God's grace.

Individual Baggage: Shadows and Compulsions

Along with the six individual gifts that you bring into your marriage, you also bring your unique individual baggage. This baggage can contort, distort, and otherwise invade your marriage, because it blocks the full and free expression of your gifts, and it undermines your spouse's expression of his or her gifts as well. We call this baggage your six "shadows" and/or your six "compulsions." These shadows and compulsions can overwhelm you with tension, and encumber both you and your spouse as you travel along the path to marital happiness. In this book, you will learn your six shadows and your six compulsions.

Shadows are places in our personality where our gifts are absent. We all have shadows. We're usually blind to our own shadows, which makes them all the more effective in blocking our gifts. Cain was acting out of his shadows rather than his gifts when he slew Abel. We are generally acting out of our shadows when we attack our spouse, whether in our behaviors or simply in our thoughts.

Compulsions are aspects of our gifts exaggerated to such a degree that they become distorted and lose their healing, soothing, and fortifying power. They are generally unconscious; we are hardly, if at all, aware of them. They sneak up on us in a stealthy manner, never knocking before they enter and do their damage. We act out of our compulsions when we force our own way in our marriage, when we insist on our own perfectionistic or idiosyncratic wants and needs over those of our spouse. We are acting out of our compulsions when we belittle or dishonor our spouse, when we ridicule his or her desires, or when we are aloof or presumptuous.

We can never eradicate our shadows or our compulsions from our lives. We can, however, become more keenly aware of them, recognize when they begin to manifest themselves, and take action to turn them around. Some of these shadows and compulsions are not at all apparent before the marriage; they only raise their heads when tension emerges and when normal interpersonal negotiation descends into contention. If these seeds of relationship damage and destruction—which may have lain fallow for years—are left to grow unpruned, they will gain even more strength and presence in our personality, and may eventually choke the life out of our marriage.

In each chapter, you will find a short self-assessment questionnaire that will give you a rough indication of your premier individual gifts. You can then find the corresponding shadows and the compulsions of those gifts in Appendix A.

I give you my own six gifts, six shadows, and six

compulsions here, simply as an example of one person's spiritual personality. My gifts assist me in my marriage, making it a place of peace, harmony, satisfaction, and holiness. My shadows and compulsions do the opposite.

Compulsion	Gift	Shadow
Presumption	Hope	Despair
Bluntness	Simplicity	Complexity
Perfectionism	Wisdom	Inadequacy
Ingratiation	Empathy	Obtuseness
Unreality	Transcendence	Worldliness
Fixation	Perseverance	Resignation

How did I identify my gifts, shadows, and compulsions? Through lots of study and personal discernment, meditation, and prayer—plus, I took the HGP3. You can learn your gifts in two ways: First, each of the next six chapters gives you a practical opportunity to subjectively identify your gifts; secondly, those who wish for a more objective method of identifying personal gifts, shadows, and compulsions can take the *Healing Gifts Profile—Third Edition* (HGP3).[2]

The goal in my marriage is to relate to my spouse from the strongest part of me, my center gifts, as much as possible. At my center stands the bedrock of my personality, the power that God has placed in me to reflect back to the world. Each of us is a reflection of Christ here on earth; we show our Christlike qualities best when we are "in" our gifts. When we function in our gifts, we are "in" love and we are "in" God. Truly, our unique giftedness all comes from love, all comes from God.

However, when I am under pressure from forces within

---

[2] The HGP3 is a scientifically constructed and validated self-assessment that generates a twenty page personal profile which identifies, defines, describes, and applies your six premier gifts, your six shadows, and your six compulsions. You can find more information about the HGP3 and all that it offers you and your spouse by logging on to the web site: www.GodHelpMyMarriage.com

myself, or more often from outside, I find myself pushed out of my gifts and pressed into my shadows and/or compulsions. When this happens, I begin to relate to my spouse from places in myself that are my "lacks," my insufficiencies, my weaknesses, my selfish ego wants. These places of insufficiency, my shadows and my compulsions, do not originate from the noblest parts of me, what Thomas Merton called my ideal self, my holy self, my real self, or my true self; rather, they originate from my false self, my worldly self, my ego self, my grabbing, arrogant, and self-absorbed self.

My unique job as a spouse is to express my gifts to Sandy. God has given me the vocation of marriage so that I can find my salvation and help Sandy find hers. I can only do this when I'm acting out of my giftedness. When Sandy and I both express our gifts, our marriage becomes an arena for happiness, personal growth, peace, wonder, awe, and delight. When I express my gifts, I am simultaneously assisting Sandy, creating the setting for her to become comfortable in expressing her gifts. When I'm expressing my gifts, I am inviting Sandy to express hers as well. In truth, I can't fully express my gifts unless and until Sandy can express her gifts as well. I'm charged with helping Sandy express her gifts, as she is charged with helping me express mine. We need each other in order to discover the wonderful truth that God has planted in each of us. We can only accomplish this by expressing our gifts.

When I am in my shadows and/or compulsions, I block Sandy from expressing her gifts. When I'm in my shadows and/or compulsions, I am, in fact "requesting" that Sandy also retreat to her shadows and compulsions. Have you ever noticed that when your spouse is in a "bad space," it usually pushes you toward a "bad space" as well? From many marital counseling sessions, I've discovered that when "bad space" is allowed to fester, the other spouse will, over time, take up a compensatory or counterbalancing "bad space." This will become clearer as we look at the "eroders" and the "evaporators" of the six marriage essentials in the following six chapters. Conversely, when your spouse is in a "good space," you generally follow suit. "Good space" is the place of our gifts. When we operate from our gifts, our spouse generally does the same. There is a dynamic reciprocity in most marriages: gifts generally beget gifts, shadows generally beget shadows, and compulsions generally beget compulsions.

2. The Couple Level: Six Essential Qualities

My professional experience, academic study, and clinical observation—together with all the mistakes, failures, and successes I've had in my own marriage—have taught me that there are *six essential qualities* that successful marriages practice on a continual basis. These six "essentials" are the fundamental competencies that successfully married people eventually discover as the bedrock of their relationships. Some are discovered by trial and error, others by stumbling upon them, as it were. Some people seem to have these qualities innately with them while others learn them through contention, negotiation, concentrated interaction, and lots of patience.

Of course, some married couples never learn them. They labor hard to give birth to marital bliss—often a painful labor full of aborted fits and false starts. Each marriage essential also has two detractors:

1. A marriage "eroder" which wears away at the relationship
2. A marriage "evaporator" which boils the spirit and life right out of the relationship

The six marriage "essentials" and the corresponding "eroders" and "evaporators" are:

Evaporator	Essential	Eroder
Enmeshment	Togetherness	Self-centeredness
Pedestaling	Respect	Resentment
Appeasement	Communication	Criticism
Possessiveness	Intimacy	Defensiveness
Blind Faith	Trust	Doubt
Codependency	Commitment	Indifference

My task in my vocation of marriage is to try to stay in the center—in the marriage essentials—as much and as often as I can, and to help Sandy do the same without dominating, manipulating, or otherwise imposing on her.

I see a lot of compensatory behavior in marriages. As one spouse retreats to either his or her eroder or evaporator, the other will begin to take the opposite position. For example— we'll see this in the many marriage examples in the next six chapters—when one spouse takes up the eroder position of "criticism," the other spouse will generally begin to gravitate toward his or her evaporator posture of "appeasement." Naturally, this leads to a very destructive environment for the couple: warmth, love, compassion, and tenderness begin to erode and evaporate away from the marriage. This is the condition in which I find most marriages when couples appear in my counseling office seeking help for their ailing relationship. They have retreated into their evaporators and eroders and individual shadows and compulsions. They feel imbalanced, insecure, disharmonious, "out of sync," angry, sad, and confused.

3. The Spiritual Level: The Couple and God

A marriage moves up to the spiritual level when spouses stay as centered as they can in their individual gifts, as well as in their marriage essentials. The spiritual level relates to the presence of God in the relationship. The more the couple level expresses itself in the six essential qualities/competencies, i.e., the more the six premier gifts of both spouses are encouraged and expressed freely, lovingly, and cleanly, the more the relationship enters the holy ground of connecting with God in the beauty of marriage. This is where the vocation of marriage springs to life, in that each partner discovers that the pathway to salvation is through the other and through their partnership.

The six spiritual conditions that will grow in your marriage as you use your individual gifts to enhance your couple level marriage essentials are listed here. Each of these will be discussed in the ensuing chapters.

1. **Sacred Unity**
2. **Spiritual Faithfulness**
3. **Transcendent Prayerfulness**
4. **Holy Groundedness**
5. **Redeeming Forgiveness**
6. **Blessed Uniqueness**

What follows in the next six chapters is a pathway that leads you step-by-step on a glorious journey of personal authenticity and marital happiness where you will discover:

- Your six unique individual gifts
- How your individual gifts can help you achieve the highest level of the six "relationship-bonding-factors" or what we call "marriage essentials"
- How you can combine your individual gifts with the six marriage essentials to catapult your marriage onto an enriching and exciting level of spiritual interaction

May you find all three dimensions in abundance, and may you discover the truth, the beauty, and the goodness in you, in your spouse, and in your marriage.

Notes

CHAPTER TWO

The First Marriage Essential: Togetherness

Let us then pursue what makes for peace and for mutual upbuilding.

ROMANS 14:19

Evaporator	Essential	Eroder
Enmeshment	Togetherness	Self-centeredness

1. The Individual Level of Togetherness

Togetherness is the first "essential" at the couple level. It is the human relationship condition created when each partner thoroughly believes she or he is an equal principal in a marriage union of common purpose. When *togetherness* is present in a marriage, each partner genuinely knows that his or her overall needs are valued as being equal to the needs of the other, thereby creating a balanced union of interdependence and a shared belief of mutuality.

Because you bring your individual gifts into your marriage, it makes sense to identify your own first individual gift before we investigate the first marriage essential any further. Your first gift, as with all six of your gifts, is your unique grace from God—the power and strength—which makes you distinctly and uniquely you. You have been given a special energy to help you in all facets of your life. Once you identify your first gift (along with its shadow and compulsion), you'll be in a privileged position to understand fully how you are addressing the couple essential quality of *togetherness*.

Individual Gifts

God is present in our lives through the work of the Holy Spirit, and the Holy Spirit works in our lives through gifts of healing and growth. These gifts provide us with the necessary energy or power to tackle the tasks of our life. We have all been uniquely gifted. We get the energy to move toward the first marriage essential of *togetherness* in and through our first individual gift.

In my research,[3] I've discovered that we each have five major individual gifts in each of the six functions of our individual personality. These gifts can be seen as the motivating power invested uniquely in you so that you can capture and successfully practice the special marital quality of *togetherness*. One of these five gifts is what I call your *premier* gift. That gift is your primary gift, the one that you favor and to which you are most attracted. To determine which of the five is your premier *togetherness* gift, review the following itemization.

Study the behavioral descriptors of the five gifts that make up the gifts of *togetherness* given on the following pages. From your review, decide which one of the five appears strongest in you. Circle this gift. You are *not* looking for the gift that you'd like to have, or that other people think you possess; rather, you are trying to identify the one gift that is most prominent in your personality *right now!*

---

[3] In an earlier book, *Body, Mind, Spirit: Tapping the Healing Power Within* (Liguori Publications, Liguori, 1992), I describe my research and the findings used to arrive at these gifts. This book describes the whole notion of individual giftedness and how the gifts fit into the six functions of your personality.

The five "togetherness gifts" are:

1. *Reliance on God*
- placing your full store of belief in God
- centering your value system in and on God
- finding your security in union with God
- feeling a strengthening certainty in and conviction of God's guiding hand
- discovering personal confidence and giving your absolute assurance to God

2. *Humility*
- requiring little to satisfy your ego needs
- being free from affectation, free from playing roles, free from projecting an image that is not genuinely you, free from wearing a mask, and free from putting on airs
- being completely honest (but not brutal) with oneself and with others
- being genuine, transparent, uncomplicated, and simple
- feeling free from worry and untainted by the cares of the world

3 *Acceptance*
- honoring the sense of being in accord with God
- positively complying with God's healing truth
- giving God your personal and complete "Amen"
- acknowledging God's supremacy and the consequent wisdom of God's plan
- seeking alignment between your own will and God's will

4. *Mercy*
- exercising leniency, forbearance, compassion, and pity
- being humane, tender, and empathic
- exhibiting humanitarian ("Good Samaritan") behavior
- having the ability to relent—to let go of judging and blaming
- granting clemency and forgiveness

5. Hope
- possessing the honest assurance that God is in charge
- having the conviction that love will remain the compelling force in life
- recognizing the promise of ultimate fairness, goodness, and cheer
- allowing yourself the perfect expectation that God's will prevails
- owning spiritual optimism and celestial confidence as your own[4]

2. The Couple Level of Togetherness

On this level, *togetherness* refers to the interdependence that a couple experiences and enjoys. Interdependence starts with the recognition that each partner in a marriage can rely upon the other and fully depend on the other. Interdependence is vastly different from both independence and dependence. Pursuing mutual independence is a trap that snares many contemporary relationships. When each partner in a marriage individually seeks his or her own personal development apart from the sacredness of the center of the marriage, *togetherness* is not growing. Dependence, on the other hand, creates an equally unhealthy relationship where one partner becomes submissive to the other, and where the needs of one partner somehow dominate the other.

Such independence or dependence will eventually result in unhappy people and anemic marriages. Gradually, but almost without exception, both partners will ultimately come to the

---

[4] Having identified the one gift that best describes you right now, turn to Appendix A. This gift is considered your "premier" individual gift on this level. It is this gift that provides you with the primary motive power to constructively address your first marriage essential of *togetherness*. In Appendix A, you'll notice that the word to the right of your premier gift is the shadow of your gift, while the word to the left of your gift is its compulsion. You may want to check Appendix B for short definitions of the shadows and the compulsions.

same conclusion: This marriage is not an honored place. The independent marriage style, in which both spouses seek their own development apart from the marriage, invariably becomes a prison for both, because each partner is eventually forced to acquiesce to the wants of the other. The independent marriage becomes a battleground for fighting over whose needs and wants will "carry the day." One partner becomes smug, the other feels dismissed. The dependent style marriage, where one partner chronically submerges his or her needs and desires to the other, results in interpersonal distance and division. The dependency figuratively takes little nicks from the body of the marriage, until eventually, if left unabated, the marriage bleeds to death.

Togetherness arises from the realization that each partner's needs and individual happiness reside in the psychological safety, support, and pleasurable interaction that only cohesiveness and mutuality can provide. Individual happiness rests on happiness as a couple. God is found in the marrow of seasoned and seasoning relationships in the *togetherness* of the relationship.

Togetherness, the felt sense of mutuality, is expressed differently in every marriage. Yet, there are commonalities of togetherness that can be identified, and which need to be exercised in order for the marriage to survive and be healthy. Look at the following characteristics of a marriage that practices *togetherness*. Ask yourself to what degree this characteristic is operating in your marriage.

When the essential couple quality of *togetherness* is present, the marriage is regarded by each partner as a place where:

- each partner has a sense of emotional and psychological safety
- there is personal peace and security
- each partner possesses a mindset of "us"

- there is equality (one spouse's needs and wants do not dominate the needs and wants of the other)
- there exists a partnership of common purpose and equally shared goals
- a healthy sense of mutuality has developed (we are a solid unit)
- partners share a genuine bond of unity or special connection
- a sense of partnership has emerged (a belief that we complement each other)
- there is cohesive, equal sharing
- there is a reciprocal emotional partnership (each spouse has the same quality of feelings for the other)

Self-centeredness—the Threat That Erodes Togetherness

One of the threats to *togetherness* is any manifestation of self-centeredness in either or both spouses. Self-centeredness is an eroder that threatens a marriage—a "place" in the marriage where the essential quality of *togetherness* is absent. If left to grow unabated, the threat of self-centeredness can gradually wear away *togetherness* to a point where it becomes too weak to support the health of the relationship.

Self-centeredness gradually undermines the stability of the marriage by pushing the needs and wants of one partner above the needs and wants of the other. A relationship imbalance can grow to a point where the relationships eventually topple.

The Self-centered Marriage

	Compulsion	Gift	Shadow
Cathy:	Self-abasement	Humility	Self-centeredness
Harry:	Presumption	Hope	Despair

Cathy and Harry's relationship had eroded into a self-centered marriage. Cathy first came into my counseling office with lots of issues surrounding her adolescent son. Cathy devoted the majority of her counseling time lamenting her son's incorrigible behaviors: how he wouldn't clean his room, how he aimlessly roamed the town in his car, his terrible grades, his lack of ambition, his thoughtlessness, etc. When I inquired about her marriage, Cathy changed her affect completely. Formerly animated and energetic when discussing her son, Cathy became submissive, retentive, even morose. While she was quite specific about her son, she was exactly the opposite about her husband Harry. Naturally, this difference struck me, and I found myself focusing on her marriage more and more, even though it was not her "ticket to counseling."

What I could put together was that Cathy's role was to serve Harry's needs. And did Harry have needs! Harry was a successful financial planner, and his priority in life was clearly his job. He selfishly demanded that all family activity revolve around his needs. He made it clear that he was simply not available for any school or recreational activities with any of the three children. Family choices in socialization, food choice, free time, television viewing—indeed all activities—were determined either directly or indirectly by Harry's preferences. Cathy was to make sure that Harry's desires became reality. This was the marriage "contract."

There was a clear relationship imbalance in this marriage. The whole belief system of the family, and especially in Cathy, exhibited a lopsided concern for Harry's desires, needs, and interests. The basic marital attitude was that Harry's needs and desires were simply more important than Cathy's or the children's needs and desires. Cathy's gift of humility had long ago contorted into self-abasement. She was so fearful of moving toward her shadow of self-centeredness that she was trapped into her contorted self-abasement, never really fully "owning" her great gift of humility.

Harry was essentially blind to anyone else's needs. He

genuinely believed that his own needs should be given prefer-ence to those of his spouse. Harry was stuck in his compulsion of presumption. "Of course," Harry reasoned, "Cathy is my wife, and she's supposed to meet my needs—that's the way a marriage should be." Psychologically, Harry was so frightened of his shadow of despair that he clung to his compulsion of presumption at all costs. His fear blocked him from getting in touch with his first gift of hope, at least in his marriage. The marriage was seriously skewed, there existed virtually no *togetherness*; indeed, it was on the verge of toppling over. It took herculean counseling work, and lots of grace from God, to bring this marriage back to some semblance of health.

> [For] those who are self-seeking and who obey not the truth but wickedness, there will be wrath and fury.
>
> ROMANS 2:8

The Dual Self-centered Marriage

	Compulsion	Gift	Shadow
Gigi:	Aloofness	Acceptance	Dissension
Ted:	Legalism	Mercy	Neglect

While Cathy and Harry's marriage was a self-centered mar-riage, it was of the single type; it was only Harry who was self-centered. A second variety of the self-centered marriage is the "dual" type where both spouses are self-centered. Ted and Gigi had such a marriage. Ted would drone on and on about finances, how the children should be disciplined, how the lawn needed raking, how their meals needed improvement, and so on. Gigi would find anything to counter Ted's increasing state-ments of discontent. Ted was caught in the compulsion of legalism, while Gigi found herself in aloofness more often than not. Naturally, their compulsions at times boomeranged them over into their shadows of dissension and neglect. These compulsion vs. shadow interactions frequently escalated into verbal "volcanic explosions." Gigi busied herself with volunteer work, childcare, friends, and her part-time job. Her complaints about Ted seemed to have no end; how he was never home, how he was inconsiderate, how he had no feelings, how he lacked social correctness, etc. Both Gigi and Ted were self-centered. As long as they stayed in this convoluted relationship posture, each new day of their marriage was doomed to be a repeat of yesterday. Their *togetherness* had eroded away.

The central problem in each of these marriages is their inability to achieve genuine *togetherness*. All four spouses were far from their central, God-given individual gift; they were alternating between their individual shadows and compulsions. Their beliefs about themselves had never made that necessary jump from being a single person to being a married team. Their attitudes and values were still in the singular mode rather than the "partnership" mode.

Marriage Evaporators

As a marriage eroder is the absence of the positive quality of the marriage essential, a marriage evaporator is an unhealthy extension of the marriage essential, a contortion of the essential which eventually distorts it into something quite different and dangerous to the health of the relationship. Marriage evaporators agitate the relationship until the essential simply boils away. As with eroders, marriage evaporators generally do their work over time; they gradually invade the integrity of the relationship by attacking the marriage essential. If steps are not taken to strengthen the foundation of the marriage, evaporators can boil the life right out of the marriage.

Enmeshment—the Evaporator of *Togetherness*

Enmeshment is a relationship condition which emerges when one (or both) partner becomes dependent on the other for making major decisions—one spouse becomes unable to move in any direction without "permission" from the other. In a sense, one partner is "too together" with the other. Generally, this is experienced by only one of the two spouses, the husband for example is enmeshed with his wife. For some reason (and there can be many), he is fearful of taking any kind of independent action, so he defers most decisions to his wife. *Togetherness* evaporates in the heat of the imbalanced relationship. In other cases, although much less common, both spouses become enmeshed in the other. In such cases neither spouse is able to take independent action without the consent of the other. Long and circular discussions arise about even small items of domestic action. Inefficiency of action marks most, if not all issues of the marriage.

Pam and Fred

	Compulsion	Gift	Shadow
Pam:	Dependency	God-reliant	Doubt
Fred:	Aloofness	Acceptance	Dissension

Pam suffers from an inability to make independent decisions. As the mother of five she has lots to do. Beyond the sheer volume of work that faces her each day, however, all decisions revolve around her husband Fred. Pam is overly entangled in the needs and wants of her children, her husband, and other extended family member as well, to the exclusion of her own needs. Pam seems captured, almost infatuated, with others to the point of a semi-slavish attachment to them, and a corresponding forfeiture of her unique self. Pam is caught in her compulsion of dependency, partly because she is fearful of her shadow of doubt. She is a most God-reliant person, yet her reliance on God is confined to moments of private prayer; she seems unable to translate the power of her giftedness into her relationship with Fred.

Fred's shadow of dissension activated Pam's dependency by making her fearful of his argumentative, demanding, and attacking demeanor. To avoid this, Pam learned to continuously "scan the horizon" of their relationship, searching for ways to please Fred in an attempt to hold him at bay. All of this had the effect of driving her ever more deeply into her compulsion and other dependent types of behavior.

Her basic personality confusion has a damaging impact on her. Pam suffers from a chronic loss of self-determination. She has become so other-directed that she has lost a healthy level of self-direction in her marriage. Pam deals with an anxious attachment to Fred—in fear of losing him, she becomes clinging, jealous, and intermittently demanding that Fred "straighten up." Yet, her protestations lack a certain sense of genuineness, definiteness, and seriousness which leaves room for the doubt that perhaps she really doesn't want Fred to change, because if he did, then she would have to change as well. Pam is caught in a conundrum of feelings, both loving and spiteful, affectionate and resentful. A marriage like this one unfortunately can stumble on for years, perhaps never finding its gifted balance. Pam is dependently enmeshed, constantly looking to Fred for personal direction and decision-making. The quality of the *togetherness* that this marriage experiences is low indeed.

3. The Spiritual Level of Togetherness

"But from the beginning of creation, 'God made them male and female. For this reason a man shall leave his father and mother and be joined to his wife, and the two shall become one flesh.' So they are no longer two, but one flesh."

MARK 10:6-8

Sacred Unity

When the condition of *togetherness* becomes sufficiently developed, it gives rise to the spiritual condition known as "sacred unity" in a relationship. Sacred unity is the spiritual relationship condition created when each partner knows without question that the marriage relationship is a diamond of wholeness, without fracture or fragmentation, joyfully reflecting the light of God.

Sacred unity refers to that relationship condition where all individual component parts of each partner are brought together by the unifying principle of God's grace. The partners live for each other without controlling one another. They fully acknowledge that the power that binds them is God. They see that they both become more than what they would be by themselves because they are not only a legal, material unit, but, indeed, a spiritual unit.

Such sacred unity can never be fully attained. We *are* broken in the sense that we are separated from God. Our earthly journey is a trek, sometimes taking us to the sunny mountaintop while at other times forcing us to stagger through the dismal swamp; nevertheless, all of it is a spiritual trek back to God. Sacred unity begins to emerge in a couple as each partner individually, yet through the other, comes to a deeper conviction of his or her inherent lovableness, i.e., "God loves me unconditionally." The binding force that creates spiritual unity—and sustains it—is love. Each spouse's first individual gift provides the power of love on this material plane which actually "does the work" of love, as it were. It is from the force of this first individual gift that sacred unity and wholeness grows into the beauty of the marital unit as a singular entity of love extension. Sacred unity enables the couple to shine as it reflects the light of Jesus and radiates the power of love which is the motivational energy of all things, animate and inanimate alike.

Sacred unity is what makes marriage a vocation and a consecration to a life of loving. The vocation and work of marriage is relationship building, because it is the relationship between the spouses—their *togetherness*—that allows love to grow. Each partner is like a love gardener, each tends the garden of the relationship so that God's love can grow there. They don't (can't) create the love between them, but they can tend the soil—water it, give it nutrients, and hoe it—so that it is much more likely to produce a bumper crop of love. Each spouse's work in the garden of the relationship fulfills Jesus' promise of life in abundance. In this way, each spouse is a minister of God, and co-creator of the harvest of love that is the fruit of the Spirit. Thus, marriage partners are only truly together when they are living, sharing, and celebrating being "in love." Sacred unity flows from *togetherness* as we more fully understand that the love relationship between marriage partners is a reflection of the love relationship between Jesus and all the children of God.

Rugged American individualism works against creating *togetherness* in marriage, and this hampers any emerging sacred unity as well. An evolving holy partnership gradually transforms us as we successively let go of our notions of ourself as simply a singular individual, and embrace values and attitudes of "coupleness" instead. The primary concern is with "us" and "we" rather than with "I" and "me." It's hard getting beyond the modern notion of marriage as a forum for self-satisfaction, toward building attitudes and values of *togetherness* and sacred unity deep within the marrow of our belief core. It's hard for us to genuinely and fully embrace that the world isn't about "me" anymore. Unless and until we can accept God's grace, however, we will miss the central point of marriage as a human institution, as well as the joy of marriage as our central spiritual development arena.

The commercial world enshrines the ego as the dominant

force of our personality. The marriage essential of *togetherness* is what gradually moves the self-seeking, narrowminded, and blinded ego away. Sacred unity further pushes the ego aside so that our interior holy self, the presence of God within us, can more fully saturate our personality with love. Egoism (self-love) and *togetherness* (spouse-love) are not happy bed partners. Marriage asks us, as God asks us, to relinquish our ego as "captain" of our personal ship, and to give the wheel, as it were, over to our interior holy self. This is where the vocation of marriage is made real, where we ultimately find joy, and where we become genuinely and authentically our true selves.

When *togetherness* is elevated to the spiritual level, we find oneness with each other. Oneness is the quality of knowing and appreciating God's grace shared between us. This oneness brings unity with God, and we begin to take on the characteristics of the ultimate lover—Jesus. Sacred unity is to realize that our purpose is to love—to reflect it and to extend it. The definition of a spouse from a *togetherness* point of view is one who brings joy and fulfillment to his or her spouse. The true joy of any spouse comes from knowing that his or her spouse is happy because he or she is expressing his/her gifts.

As married people, we find our own unity with God in the sacred unity of our marriage. This is the essence of our spiritual life journey across the life span:

- to purge ourselves of whatever separates us from God (our shadows and compulsions)
- to illuminate our minds with the recognition of love in relationship
- to find unity with God by reflecting God's love in our world

We can never accomplish these fully, but through our vocation of marriage we can come closer and closer each day. *Togetherness* and sacred unity is about two people but one entity: not about two separate satisfactions, but one; not about two separate fulfillments, but one; not about two distinct "happinesses," but only one!

Notes

CHAPTER THREE

The Second Marriage Essential: Respect

For the wife does not have authority over her own body, but the husband does; likewise the husband does not have authority over his own body, but the wife does.

1 CORINTHIANS 7:4

Evaporator	Essential	Eroder
Pedestaling	Respect	Resentment

1. The Individual Level of Respect

First, a definition of "respect": The human relationship condition created when each partner sees the uniqueness of the other. Each partner's personal specialness is honored and cherished by the other partner as a part of the gift of the marriage.

As in chapter two, before exploring this second marriage essential, try first to identify your premier "respect gift." Identify *one* of the five gifts listed on the following pages as your premier *respect* gift, first by studying the descriptors under each of the gifts and then intuitively identifying which one of the five is most operative in your life right now.

The five "respect gifts" are:

1. Vision

- seeing the world through the eyes of God
- possessing the clear awareness that there is another realm beyond the physical
- the ability to catch a glimpse of heaven right here on earth
- the power to discern God's glory in the daily events of your life
- viewing the light of heaven shining from behind the actions of humanity

2. Humor

- discovering, expressing, or appreciating the ludicrous or absurdly incongruous
- finding comical or amusing cheer in the human existence
- finding levity in oneself by taking a completely objective viewpoint
- recognizing the light side—seeing delight, exultation, revelry, and jubilation
- being optimistic and sparkling

3. Peace

- listening to the great quiet within you
- finding harmony and concord in virtually everything you encounter
- knowing you live in God's celestial security and serenity
- living in a state where love abides
- that gift of tranquility one receives when God's plan (as opposed to yours) for happiness is finally and fully accepted

4. Adaptability

- conforming in spiritually growth-filled ways to God's precepts
- taking on the ways of Christ—adopting God's will

- converting oneself from the separation the world teaches to the brilliance and unity that heaven teaches
- harmonizing oneself with heaven
- adjusting to being in the world but not of this world

5. *Simplicity/Beauty*
- being exquisitely open and childlike
- possessing a naive gracefulness, loveliness, and charm
- having the qualities of radiance and magnificence
- having no pretense, being uncomplicated and innocent
- being someone who brings pleasure that is clean, delicate, elegant, and glorious[5]

2. The Couple Level of Respect

Years ago, the gospel singer Aretha Franklin reminded us of one of the central ingredients of any successful relationship when she recorded her famous song *Respect*. In a marriage, *respect* means recognizing the uniqueness of one's spouse and acting in ways which fully cherish that person as a unique individual who is made, quite purposefully by God, to be just who he or she is.

It's strange that the very thing that originally brought the couple together, the beautiful differences that exist between each of the partners, is sometimes so quickly discounted as the marriage unfolds its uniqueness. *Respect* does not mean simply tolerance of an unwanted "difference" one partner may see in the other. *Respect* means holding up this difference as a part of the celestial beauty of this person. The opposite of *respect* is being judgmental, which ultimately breeds resentment, and even contempt.

---

[5] Once you have identified the *one* gift that best describes you right now in your life, then turn to Appendix A. Your chosen gift is considered your "premier" individual gift on the *respect* level. It is this "gift" that provides you with the primary motive power to positively and constructively address your second marriage essential of *respect*. In Appendix A, you'll notice that the word to the right of your premier gift is the shadow of your gift, while the word to the left of your gift is its compulsion. See Appendix B for a review of shadows and compulsions.

Respect also goes beyond giving "credit where credit is due" by going to the heart of the love relationship. *Respect* means coming to genuinely know, appreciate, and even honor the unique giftedness of one's spouse, and holding up this specialness as a manifestation of God's love and care for the marriage.

A facet of *respect* is honoring even what you don't like about your spouse, cherishing some of the things that he or she does that usually annoy you, and even revering some behaviors that formerly agitated you. This does not mean that you now "like" these behaviors or characteristics; it only means that you have grown to love your spouse so much in the spirit of *respect* that you now find these formerly disliked characteristics, behaviors, or quirks endearing rather than repelling. It's a strange paradox when you see this happening in your marriage, but make no mistake about it: It is the great power of *respect* at work—the keystone of a seasoned or seasoning marriage.

When the quality of *respect* is present, the marriage is regarded by each partner as a place where:

- each partner's unique personal identity is honored
- each partner's "personhood" is allowed to be expressed
- each partner genuinely accepts the personal idiosyncrasies or quirks of the other
- each partner is free to pursue personal growth so long as it does not violate the *togetherness* of the marriage
- each partner in the marriage is the person most important to the other
- confidences are honored completely
- a distinctively reverent familiarity exists in the marriage
- each partner is cherished by the other in word and action (to the point where even the actions that are *not* liked by one are still cherished)
- unconditional positive regard, the healing quality of love, is practiced in the marriage

- each spouse gives affirmation to the other as a daily marital action

Resentment—the Eroder of Respect

Rid yourselves, therefore, of all malice, and all guile, insincerity, envy, and all slander.

1 PETER 2:1

Resentment is a directly or indirectly expressed feeling—but always expressed—of displeasure or persistent ill will at something regarded as a wrong, insult, injury, or otherwise emotionally hurtful wound. Oftentimes, resentment can emerge in a relationship as a consequence of "carry overs" from childhood. Childhood experiences of being chronically frightened, or being labeled "irresponsible" can breed personalities that are immature, dependent, intolerant, frustrated, critical, angry, etc. This is not to say that all resentment is caused by childhood deficiencies, but when resentment does grow in a marriage, it calls for a review and analysis of childhood experiences. Resentment arises in a marriage when *respect* has been violated. Consider the marriage of Ed and Debbie.

The Resentful Marriage

	Compulsion	Gift	Shadow
Debbie:	Appeasement	Peace	Contention
Ed:	Illusion	Vision	Blindness

Ed was an up-and-coming executive with designs on becoming president of his corporation. He had married Debbie when she was still in high school; he, on the other hand, had already graduated from college. Ed was ambitious and wanted a wife who would put him on a pedestal. He was the only son of an alcoholic father. This incomplete role model, who couldn't nurture his son, left Ed feeling empty, affectively distant from his own feelings, and in need of someone who would always look up to him as a savior. Debbie, on the other hand, was from a close-knit family with no history of higher education. Debbie was dazzled by Ed's charm, confidence, ambition, and relentless courting of her. She fell for him because she was so flattered that someone from his "social level" would see her as a potential life partner. His strong personality gave her confidence, and she knew that Ed would far outpace the economic level of her family.

For the first ten years of the marriage, the strict division of responsibilities in the marriage, and the dominant-submissive roles, were carried out by both spouses to the letter. As Debbie gained more maturity and more experience with the kinds of relationships that her friends and neighbors had in their marriages, she gradually became discontent with her constricted relationship with Ed. She longed to become free, to express herself, to take risks, and to learn who she really was. The more she tried to do this, the more Ed protested.

Debbie's second individual gift is peace, yet for the first ten years of the marriage, she had lived almost exclusively in the compulsion of appeasement. Now she was heading for the shadow of contention. Ed would ridicule, chastise, criticize, and bully her "into place." Although not physically abusive, he certainly was so, verbally and emotionally. He was stuck in his compulsion of illusion in seeing himself as most important, and in his shadow of blindness with regard to Debbie's needs.

As Ed's verbal attacks escalated, Debbie found her feelings toward Ed changing. Her former respect for her husband, her pride in his accomplishments, their nice home, his ease in social situations, etc., was turning into an ever growing resentment. By the time she found her way to my counseling office, her resentment had evolved into contempt. She was beginning to hate her husband. She would look at him and see evil—a slave master, a jailer, a tormentor who would stop at nothing to get his way. When resentment sours into contempt, it's a most ominous sign; without strong intervention, the marriage is usually headed for disaster. In the end, when Ed realized that Debbie, despite his threats, was leaving the relationship, he relented and didn't contest the divorce. Debbie was awarded full custody of their three children. She eventually gained some level of emotional and financial stability, but it took a very long time. In the interim, Debbie struggled with her decision to end the marriage, she suffered with dramatically conflicting feelings, and with her lack of emotional maturity, which she ultimately realized had hobbled the relationship since the beginning of their marriage.

Some of Debbie's feelings and behaviors of resentment were expressed in irritation and annoyance, taking offense, bristling and flaring up, pouting, frowning, scowling, snapping, fuming, seething, and bursting with anger. She also suffered feelings of animosity, indignation, exasperation, and bitterness. Some of Ed's feelings and behaviors in the marriage expressed themselves as provoking, incensing, rebuffing, arousing anger, and offending Debbie by slighting and/or discounting her, especially with respect to any particular accomplishment of hers.

The interplay between these two spouses became white-hot; it scorched the life out of the marriage and fostered division and distance, thus obliterating closeness, tenderness, and loving care. Before the end, Debbie had stopped praying for a marital transformation; she was praying for a harmonious divorce.

Pedestaling—the Evaporator of Respect

Each of us is originally drawn to our partner because we see in him or her ways in which we ourselves can be fulfilled. We may not even be aware that we perceive in this potential spouse the hope of personal completeness, satisfaction, personal meaning, and a lifelong purpose. We somehow see in our potential spouse some competency, potential, ability, and possession that we believe we need or want. In a generalized way, we could say that we see in our potential spouse something that we respect, even revere very much.

I fell in love with Sandy because I saw in her a very loyal person, a person who could flower with me and I with her, a person who could fulfill my dreams for affection, attention, nurturance, harmony, and connection. I saw a person who was easy to talk with, shared my value system, had immense personal integrity and faith, and who was not afraid to work. All of these—and I'm sure many more that I was not fully aware of at the time, since I'm constantly gaining new awareness of the beautiful gift that is Sandy—were somehow mixed together in my mind, heart, and soul. These characteristics were seasoned with immense physical attraction, desire, and need; they all combined to create the absolutely perfect life/love partner for me.

Each of us has a different list of requisites—conscious or not—of what's important for us in a spouse. This list, which is sometimes very short, is what constitutes our *respect* for the other person. This list also begins to generate expectations of what this potential spouse should be like in the marriage. Some have lists that begin and end with sex, money, or power; for others, it's intelligence, coming from a "good" family, or the "right" religion, etc. When a list contains one issue or characteristic that seems to tower above the others, outside onlookers sometimes use the word "seduce" to describe the intense attraction felt by one potential partner for the other, because this person was seduced by the singular issue or characteristic that dominated his or her own list. The word we will use to describe such a single-issue desire in a potential spouse is "pedestaling." Let's look at Cindy and Roger.

The Pedestaling Marriage

	Compulsion	Gift	Shadow
Cindy:	Illusion	Vision	Blindness
Roger:	Recklessness	Humor	Lamentation

Cindy respected intellectual activity too much—she pedestaled it. Intellectual achievement meant everything to her, and she was willing to sacrifice all else for it. She was supremely intelligent herself, and came from a family where intellectual achievement was the dominant personal trait elevated above all others. Cindy revered education, degrees, and academic accomplishments. She already had a Ph.D. in philosophy and was looking for a life mate who could stimulate her thinking, excite her brain, probe her intelligence with his own, and generally be a cognitive sparing partner. Eventually, she found a man who was clearly brilliant. He was so bright that he even thought of himself as more intelligent than Cindy.

Cindy was so "turned-on" by Roger's brilliance that he seduced her with it. This could only happen because Cindy had put his intellectual abilities and prowess on a pedestal. Perceiving Roger through a very thick pair of rose-colored glasses—and her own need for an intellectual partner—she was blinded to all the other qualities she wanted in a spouse. Roger lived up to every intellectual desire she had. Their conversations were so animated, dramatic, and wonderful that she never wanted them to end.

Roger felt the same way, but he had distorted his gift of humor to such a degree that he had descended into the compulsion of recklessness when he engaged in arguments. Roger was terrified by his shadow of lamentation which at times had made him depressed.

For several months all went extremely well. Cindy found in Roger all that she ever wanted. Soon, however, storm clouds descended over the intellectually vibrant dialogues and the relationship that they had constructed. The back-and-forth of their discussions began to take on a more heated tone, then an edge, then accusations—all stated with logic and supported by chapter and verse of back-up material to prove every point. Their sparkling discussions, which were formerly fun and exciting, began to take on a quality of biting criticism and superiority.

Worst of all, Cindy and Roger seemed powerless to temper their discussions when the heat began to rise. Discussions escalated into arguments, arguments into tirades, and tirades slowly took a turn toward the physical. First there was simply physical posturing; Cindy would "get in Roger's face," and Roger would push his larger body against hers. Then one night, Cindy became so incensed at what she considered Roger's insensitivity and haughty accusations that she actually slapped him. Several times their arguments became so heated that neighbors actually called the police. Roger even spent a night in jail. Cindy had gone beyond even pedestaling; she had become possessed. Things had gotten out of hand. When she finally showed up in my counseling office, all Cindy could say after describing the latest altercation between her and Roger was, "But he's so bright."

3. The Spiritual Level of Respect

Happy is the husband of a good wife; the number of his days will be doubled. A loyal wife brings joy to her husband, and he will complete his years in peace. A good wife is a great blessing; she will be granted among the blessings of the man who fears the Lord. Whether rich or poor, his heart is content, and at all times his face is cheerful.

SIRACH 26:1-4

Spiritual Faithfulness

When the condition of *respect* emerges in a relationship, this facilitates the birth of "spiritual faithfulness." Spiritual faithfulness is created in a marriage when each partner sees and recognizes with certainty that God is the center of the marriage, making it a holy bond.

Faith gives us a confident loyalty to God. It allows us a strong conviction in the presence of God's guiding hand. Faith means adhering firmly to our genuine spiritual nature. Faith builds us up, fear tears us down. Faith places God at the center of a marriage and generates fidelity with our spouse and our marriage. Faith is to a marriage what sails are to a ship: not a burden but a means of energy. Spiritual faithfulness empowers us to see our spouse through the eyes of Christ, to see the love that drives this person, the truth, beauty, and goodness placed there by God.

A marriage in which the spouses do not have faith in each other—as well as faith that God is at the center of the relationship—is a marriage that will have a hard time sustaining itself in a world that places a high premium on individual freedom while discounting individual responsibility and accountability. When faith and trust drains from a marriage, little is left. This is why forgiveness is so immensely important in any marriage. Forgiveness allows God's love to become as perennial as the spring grass.

A singular perspective is not *respect*-full. When we function on the level of, "I just want to be me," we miss the point of marriage. When this happens, we're only perceiving one side of the equation, and we act like one oar in the water, one hand clapping, one prong on the electrical plug. When we don't put faith in the relationship through God, or when we are disrespectful of each other, no spark of love can flow to and through the relationship. Only when we succeed in seeing our self as one of two prongs of the plug, do the gates open to let love rush in.

When *respect* grows into faithfulness, we see our marriage as our primary vocation. Our profession, trade, or job is secondary to the primacy of our spousal responsibilities. *Respect* means that our love is irrevocable, "I can never renege on my love to you; I can never put anything or anyone else before my love for you; I cannot take my love back from you." *Respect* means that I continuously strive to achieve the very best in and for my marriage. I am charged with nothing short of aiming for greatness in my marriage, not simply avoiding failure. I need God's grace to keep a positive mental attitude, certainly about my spouse, but also about my role in the relationship. When I become dispirited, irritated, sharp, flippant, and otherwise self-absorbed, I am violating the *respect* of the marriage and blocking spiritual faithfulness.

My choice of Sandy as my lifelong partner means I am called to respect her above all else. Whenever I perceive what I think Sandy "should do" or "could be," I am being fundamentally disrespectful of who and what she *is*. The grace of marriage calls me to respect her and to have faith in her, not in the "should" or "could" of my own silly reckoning of her. Faithfulness means that Sandy and I are linked heart and soul like nothing else.

CHAPTER FOUR

The Third Marriage Essential: Communication

Evaporator	Essential	Eroder
Appeasement	Communication	Criticism

1. The Individual Level of Communication

First, a definition of "communication": The human relationship condition created when each partner uses the language of caring and compassion, spends quality time with his or her partner, and works out the inevitable differences that emerge in all relationships by using healing interaction skills.

Before you explore the third marriage essential, identify your premier "communication gift." Identify *one* of the five gifts listed below as your primary gift of *communication*, first by studying the descriptors under each of the gifts and then intuitively identifying which one of the five gifts is most operative in your life right now. Consult Appendix A for the shadows and the compulsions of your chosen gift.

The five "communication gifts" are:

1. Faith
- being loyal to God and confident in God's sustaining power
- having strong conviction in God's guiding hand

- possessing resolute and obedient fidelity to God
- "owning" a personally functional creed with God at its center
- adhering in a staunch and firm way to one's genuine (spiritual) nature

2. Wisdom

- using accumulated knowledge well
- discerning God's presence and/or spiritual qualities in others
- possessing an illuminated, enlightened and solid insight, good sense, judgment
- being spiritually intuitive
- recognizing the most prudent, sane, and sensible course

3. Love

- unselfishly seeing God in everyone
- thriving on giving adoration to God
- holding dear to your heart the holiness, blessedness, and the wholeness in the world as a reflection of God's pure love
- prizing God above all else
- unwavering benevolence toward God's children

4. Wholeness

- the state of being intact, complete, integrated
- being entirely undiminished—an unbroken unit
- possessing the quality of concentration toward one goal
- feeling united with God
- achieving togetherness with God and God's ways

5. Charity

- having unconditionally benevolent good will
- giving without expecting anything in return
- working to help other people in a selfless manner

- recognizing the needs of another and giving in a big-hearted manner
- possessing and using forgiveness and altruism[6]

2. The Couple Level of Communication

You must understand this, my beloved: let everyone be quick to listen, slow to speak, slow to anger; for your anger does not produce God's righteousness.

JAMES 1:19-20

How many times have you heard that the reason a particular marriage failed was due to "lack of communication"? The kind of communication that a marriage thrives on is called "facilitative communication." Essentially, this means that each spouse actively practices certain communication skills that have been found to enhance and encourage interaction between two people who truly care about one another.

The primary facilitative communication skills are:

1. Active Listening: Giving focused attention to the speaker.
2. Attending to the feelings underlying the words of one's spouse, thereby understanding the full meaning of what is being said.
3. Valuing and focusing upon both the message itself and the message sender.
4. Speaking for oneself, rather than speaking for one's spouse.

---

[6] Identify the one gift that best describes you right now, then turn to Appendix A. Your chosen gift is your "premier" individual *communication* gift. It is this "gift" that provides you with the primary motive power to positively and constructively address your third marriage essential of *communication*. In Appendix A, the shadow of your gift is the word to the right of your gift, and your compulsion is the word to the left of it. Appendix B contains short definitions of each of the shadows and compulsions.

5. Being able to freely express feelings and being confident that they will be accepted by one's spouse in emotional safety.

6. Encouraging one's spouse to talk without nagging him or her.

7. Providing constructive feedback (not criticism) to one's spouse after she/he has given a message.

Once again, healthily seasoned and seasoning relationships have found ways of accomplishing some or all of these skills on a consistent basis.

A communicative marriage:

- deals constructively with misunderstandings
- exercises honesty in thought and word
- shows genuineness (what you see and what I say is genuinely who I am)
- gives time so that full communication can take place
- explores the emotional depth and the personal breadth of one another
- makes room for spending quality time together
- enjoys each other's expression of self as well as the relationship itself
- listens...listens...listens, and listens some more
- works toward resolving conflict in a win-win way—no victor and no loser
- expresses feelings constructively and positively, even if the feelings are negative ones

Criticism—the Eroder of Communication

"Do not judge, so that you may not be judged. For with the judgment you make you will be judged, and the measure you give will be the measure you get."

MATTHEW 7:1-2

We are being critical when we think that all we're doing is pointing out the "right" thing. Many times I have heard in marriage counseling sessions, "I just want to do the 'right' thing." I've learned that this is actually a statement of a critical spouse who carries the idea that his or her way is the "right" way—the best way for everyone involved. The statement also carries a strong overtone that the spouse should "see the light" of this "superior" thinking.

The adage, "Would you rather be right or would you rather be happy?" is particularly cogent in marriages. We certainly want to do what is right, yet when we push for what is "right" according to our own thinking, we may be unaware of how disrespectfully damaging it is to the marriage essential of *togetherness*. Pushing for what is right rarely brings ultimate happiness—indeed, it usually brings the opposite. Your spouse comes to believe that you are a bully, perceives you as an immature child who just wants his or her "way," feels subjugated and angry, chooses (usually unconsciously) to avoid you, and enters into behavior best described as withdrawal or passive-aggressive. You may "win the battle" of being right, but you are certainly setting yourself up to "lose the war" of a happy marriage.

We are being critical when we:

- reprehend, blame, censure, reprobate, condemn, denounce
- judge, reprove, examine, dissect, analyze, review
- roast, offer no affirmation or no compliment, only see the bad, see everything as needing improvement, cast a critical eye
- lack acceptance, are never satisfied, claim that something's always wrong
- press guilt upon our spouse, or charge him or her with ineptitude or shortcomings of some sort

- attempt to apply mathematical or scientific logic to a human situation
- attempt to prove our opinion as correct, and therefore superior, by virtue of logic
- expose the thinking of our spouse as inferior or lacking in some crucial ingredient
- argue that our logic is superior to the other (when both spouses think their "logic" is superior, what emerges is the marital game of "who's right?" or "I'm right and you're wrong!")
- assume the posture of a judge, determining or pronouncing after inquiry or deliberation, chronically giving an authoritative opinion

The Critical Marriage

Unfortunately, the critical marriage is more common that one might think. There are several variations of the critical marriage.

The "Who is Right?" Critical Marriage

	Compulsion	Gift	Shadow
Kent:	Servitude	Charity	Judgment
Jackie:	Perfectionism	Wisdom	Inadequacy

Jackie and Kent were at it again. Kent had just related to Jackie about something that occurred at work that day when she pounced on him with, "What made you say that?" Immediately, Kent leapt to the defensive, as he had done thousands of times before. His immediate reaction was to justify his response to her. "Well, any logical person would have acted the same way!" "No, they wouldn't! A logical person would have said...", asserts Jackie. The interchange drones on and on, with no real communication evolving, each simply stabbing at the other with independent statements said in reaction, not response to the spouse. It's the game of "Who is right?" at its worst.

Both Jackie and Kent have fallen into an interchange pattern that originates from either their shadows or their compulsions, rather than from their gifts. Jackie is stuck in her shadow of perfectionism, while Kent uses his shadow of judgment. Their respective gifts of wisdom and charity are covered over. In a marriage like this, where both spouses "come at each other" either from their shadows or from their compulsions, each is "forcing" the spouse to respond in kind. This unfortunate pattern not only blocks true communication, it severs togetherness and respect at the same time.

The "Violations of Self-Esteem" Critical Marriage

	Compulsion	Gift	Shadow
Carol:	Sentimentality	Love	Fear
Bill:	Parochial	Wholeness	Fragmented

"Why do you always put the butter on the toast like that?" snaps Bill. The question descends like a club out of nowhere. Carol, his wife, with her back to him, simply rolls her eyes, as she realizes that her husband has just started again. "You don't even know how to butter toast, don't you know how to do anything?" says Bill, attackingly. Once again, Carol says nothing. Bill continues, "You just can't learn, can you? I don't know how you graduated from high school, let alone college. Of course, anybody could have gotten a degree in the courses you took."

Bill's criticism has only one purpose—to undermine Carol. His goal is not to correct her as much as it is to attack her very sense of self. He jabs at her self-esteem again and again, like a boxer circling his opponent, attempting to weaken her little by little until she simply falls over in exhaustion.

Carol's sentimentality pushes her to always want things to be "nice." This causes her to overlook, or at least brush aside, Bill's terrible criticism. His critical nature comes from his compulsion of parochialism, which makes him see only one small part of any situation and not see the whole of it. This marriage needs to find its center of peace and harmony, its gifts of love and wholeness.

The "Judgment Business" Critical Marriage

	Compulsion	Gift	Shadow
Joan:	Overzealousness	Faith	Disloyalty
Rocco:	Perfectionism	Wisdom	Inadequacy

Joan and Rocco truly love each other, but they have never learned how to communicate their love to one another. Instead, they appear as though they are in the "judgment business." Almost everything that either one of them utters is subject to an immediate assessment, evaluation, and a final judgment. True conversation isn't allowed in their marriage, interchange is a matter of putting everything under the microscope of criticism. Both Joan and Rocco have become accomplished critics of each other. Expressions of love, facilitative communication, statements of confirmation, and simple requests for clarification are absent from their dialogue.

Joan relates to Rocco mainly through her overzealousness; her passionate approach to life injects a sense of urgency, necessity, and even a demanding quality to her words. Rocco reacts to his wife mainly through his compulsion of perfectionism. For Rocco, everything must be right, and Joan's tendency to overstate issues in an emotional way catapults Rocco into a counterbalancing tirade in her ongoing attempt to gain the upper hand in the relationship. His perfectionism is driven by his shadow of inadequacy. For Rocco, the worst anxiety provoking situation is to come across as somehow inadequate, incapable, or insufficient. Rocco has built his personality on being capable, resourceful, and a cut above everyone else. In his heart of hearts, however, Rocco feels that he's somewhat of an imposter and fears being exposed for what he fears about himself. As a cover up, Rocco projects an "I know best" image, which only imprisons him in his compulsion of perfectionism and forces him into a life of criticism.

The "Attack—Attack" Critical Marriage

	Compulsion	Gift	Shadow
Mary:	Servitude	Charity	Judgment
Steve:	Servitude	Charity	Judgment

Unlike Joan's and Rocco's marriage—where they do love each other—Mary's and Steve's marriage is devoid of love. Somewhere along the line, whatever love they once shared has leached out of their marriage, leaving it empty. Their conversation is not communication at all, however; it's really an exchange of "attacks." Because they can't face up to this reality, Mary and Steve carry on a charade-like relationship where both project their anger at each other in day-to-day conversation. They are relentless in finding ways of cutting the other down. The sparring can escalate into an argument, and the argument typically descends into an exchange of attacks. The attacks are nondiscriminatory and sloppy attempts at releasing the intense emotions that are stored up in them. Each blasts the other without mercy.

Notice that Mary and Steve share the same gift in this third marriage essential, and thus they share the same shadow and compulsion as well. It's fairly easy to see that their attacking ways are borne from their shadow of being judgmental. Psychologically, both Mary and Steve are fearful of their compulsion of servitude. They both fear that their marriage will force them into slavish subjugation from which they can't escape. This unfortunate underlying, and probably unconscious, tendency devalues their marriage, robbing it of the other marriage essentials as well. The only antidote they have is to fully "own" their mutual gift of charity. This is where they will find the energy necessary to surmount the devastating abyss of attack into which they have fallen. Only this spiritual power, however they tap into it, can allow this marriage to find its loving ways.

Appeasement—the Evaporator of Communication

The Appeasing Marriage

	Compulsion	Gift	Shadow
Karen:	Sentimentality	Love	Fear
Jim:	Parochialism	Wholeness	Fragmentation

Karen and Jim have settled into the classically appeasing marriage: Karen is the appeaser, while Jim is the critic. Shortly after their wedding, Karen was shocked to realize that the man she thought she married had somehow "evaporated." Jim's whole demeanor changed; his former attentiveness to Karen's positive traits completely changed into a focus on what he thought Karen needed to change. Jim's formerly affirming nature turned to attack, and his former courteousness flipped to curtness. Karen was flabbergasted, and she didn't know what to do. She was young, and her belief was that marriage was for a lifetime. She thought that if she made the marriage "work," the real Jim would surely return. She embarked on a program to "kill Jim with kindness." Karen overlooked Jim's nagging, his quips, and his slights. Instead, she concentrated on all his good points. She told him what she wanted to hear from him about her. She would constantly build him up, point out his positive points, say "nice" things, and focus only on his needs. She became a regular appeaser, allowing herself to see only the good; all else she would simply dismiss from her mind.

When Jim would point out something he didn't like about

Karen, she would artificially placate him by mollifying his accusations with concessions. She found herself saying more and more words like, "Oh, you're right dear. Don't worry about that, I'll take care of that tomorrow." She would appease his discontent. She would pacify him, settle, make excuses, and "buy him off" with diversions of all sorts, both verbal and physical. Sex became a tool she would use to divert him, more than an expression of communicative love.

As this continued, and especially when she realized that Jim's behavior was not improving, but indeed getting worse, Karen became more and more disappointed, dispirited, and finally depressed. Karen had moved from her compulsion of sentimentality over into her shadow of fear. It was her fear of her shadow that had kept Karen in the appeaser mode for so long. Jim was obviously displeased about her depression. He moved into his shadow of fragmentation. Unable to see the whole picture of what Karen was experiencing, his thinking regarding Karen became more and more fragmented. "Why aren't you like you used to be?" he would blurt out. "You've changed!" he would exclaim, as though this was all Karen's problem and he was completely uninvolved in her flattened mood. It was a real testimony to Karen's strength that she held out like this for ten years. With each of her three pregnancies and the birth of her children, Karen's gift of love would buoy her up, only to be dashed once again when Jim still didn't change his ways. Finally, when Karen thought she couldn't go on, she sought out a counselor. The counselor explained that her first step was to "work" on herself. First of all, she needed to get herself emotionally healthy, then she could begin to work on the marriage.

The Ingratiating Marriage—a Variation of Appeasement

	Compulsion	Gift	Shadow
Maddy:	Parochialism	Wholeness	Fragmentation
Phil:	Overzealousness	Faith	Disloyalty

Maddy and Phil seemed the ideal couple. They had three beautiful daughters, and lived in a very comfortable home made possible by Phil's job. They participated in many community, church, political, and social organizations and events. They belonged to three recreational clubs: golf, tennis, and a swim club. Whatever was offered in their community, Maddy and Phil seemed first in line. Maddy was exceedingly self-confident, determined, and strong-willed; some might even call her opinionated. She was very bright and quick-tongued; she could craft a well thought out answer for any issue or question that came her way with ease. Socially charming, conversational, quick-witted, and physically attractive, Maddy was noticed when she entered a room and remembered when she left.

Phil was quite the opposite. A star athlete and strikingly handsome, he was "Mr. Laid Back." He seemed unflappable, easy going, humorous, and calm. Phil was everyone's friend; indeed, there was nothing about Phil that wasn't likeable. He never ruffled anyone; he was ever agreeable, ever compliant, ever flexible. Maddy got many compliments from her friends about her husband Phil; they just loved him. To them, Phil seemed like the husband they wished they had. Phil seemed to have no flaws. Yet underneath the artificial veneer of this public image lay an angst, a pain that was hidden, hard to define, and destructive for the marriage.

In their private lives, the picture of the happy, agreeable couple was very far away indeed. They never fought, nor did they disagree, but make no mistake about the fact that Maddy was the undisputed head of the family. Her word was law. She never appeared to neglect or abuse Phil; that wasn't Maddy's style. Rather, she maintained the upper hand through sheer determination, logic, and perseverance. "Phil, wouldn't it be nice if we had a new backyard garden?" "Phil, hon, what about a skiing vacation, just the two of us; well, and of course the Oswalds and the Romanos—we'd have such a good time." Even though these seemed like requests, Maddy had a way of making a request appear like a demand. Although Phil didn't agree with her, he would, nevertheless, feel stupid, naked, alone, and undefended. Maddy wasn't demanding, per se, but her thoughts were posed in such a way that if Phil didn't agree, Maddy would bear down on him like a prosecuting attorney on the attack, making him justify his thinking and his position. She was so adept at countering Phil's thoughts with her quick wit and superior verbal skills that, in the end, Phil would simply acquiesce.

Maddy was dauntless in her tenacious control over Phil. She treated Phil not so much as her husband as like a hired hand. She acted kindly toward him like one would act kindly toward one's dog or cat. Her kindliness, however, was simply a front, designed to hoodwink even herself into thinking that she really loved Phil, when actually her self-absorption blocked a genuine understanding of love. Her fragmented thinking created a "logic" that was lopsided, self-centered, and wholly focused on her own needs. Maddy had always gotten her way. As a consequence, she never came to own her gift of wholeness, but contorted it into a parochial compulsion, seeing only a small part of a much larger picture. The small part she was consumed with was her own welfare, her own logic, her own idiosyncratic way of making sense of the world. She was sure to always compliment Phil in public, but in private she ran the family and the marriage on a schedule and with rules that would put any drill sergeant to shame. Phil was simply one of the many pieces in Maddy's life that she was charged with manipulating so that all and everything ran efficiently, efficaciously, and smoothly according to her well designed plans.

Over time, Phil learned to "toe the line." He feared his shadow of disloyalty. His family of origin was very stable—no divorces, no hint of breakup, no contention, only stability and loyalty. Phil was at his core a faithful guy. Yet Maddy's personality flaws were enough to undo him. Unfortunately, he flew to his compulsion of overzealousness. He became overly agreeable. Nothing that Maddy said was wrong in any way, at least not publicly. Phil flattered Maddy, fawned over her, ingratiated himself to her. Phil learned to appease her; when she asked for something, he wouldn't disagree, but simply become silent, which Maddy took as agreement. Phil learned to pacify Maddy. If she wanted a new ski outfit, he would say that was a fine idea. He didn't actually weigh the decision, he simply agreed. Phil would conciliate, he would "buy off" Maddy, usually forfeiting himself along the way. To placate her, he might put on a show of arranging for a romantic sexual liaison later in the evening, only to "forget" as the evening progressed. He would mollify her with concessions, "Well, I can't do that this weekend, but I'll be sure to get it done next weekend." Phil began finding more and more ways of leaving the house. He joined men's clubs, and eventually became an officer so that there were more meetings. Phil became passive-aggressive: forgetting, being late, sublimating his growing anger into physical activities—becoming an accomplished golfer, for example. Phil was slowly losing his very self to his spouse's dominant ways, and the marriage was slowly unraveling. Their marriage lacked honest, genuine, and heartfelt communication.

3. The Spiritual Level of Communication

Husbands, in the same way, show consideration for your wives
in your life together, paying honor to the woman as the weaker
sex, since they too are also heirs of the gracious gift of life—so
that nothing may hinder your prayers.

1 PETER 3:7

Transcendent Prayerfulness

When the condition of *communication* emerges in a relationship, the birth of "transcendent prayerfulness" is facili-
tated. The spiritual relationship condition created in a marriage, when each partner thinks of marriage as an ongoing
communication with God, becomes for both a journey of faith
with God.

Prayerfulness is the natural spiritual extension of honesty
and *communication*. Prayerful couples are communicating with
God. We can accomplish nothing on our own—we continuously need God's assistance. For this reason we pray—on our
own and with our spouse. When we pray, we open ourselves
up to God's grace in ways not possible without prayer. Prayer
enhances us because it reminds us of who we really are: children of God. And when we pray for our spouse, we bring our
marriage closer together as we are enabled to see the beauty of
our spouse more clearly.

Praying together lends a blessing to all the other characteristics of the marriage. Praying together opens up the marriage,
and positions it in such a way that it can better receive the full
measure of the grace that God showers upon it. Praying
together enhances the immediacy in the marriage—a felt sense
that we are right here, right now with one another; there is no
sense of absence or even distance. Seasoned and seasoning
relationships can actually grow into a union that is an ongoing

prayer. Each partner is consistently mindful of the fact that his/her partner is God's child and God's love in action—a graced presence to be honored like none other. Seasoned and seasoning relationships pray!

Prayer can spell the difference between personal growth and stagnation, between energizing development and lifeless inertia, and between spiritual vibrancy and a shallow emptiness in our relationship. Prayer is *the* constant force promoting all six essentials of a happy, healthy, and holy marriage.

Prayer sustains us in our marriage because it moves us toward our most noble parts and allows us to express and understand these God-given gifts in us and between us. Prayer inspires a marriage with a perspective that takes the couple beyond "surface" communication into communion with God. Our capacity for recognizing and receiving the grace of God is clearly connected with our prayer life. Prayer allows us to pause so we can detach from the daily routines of life and find spiritual refreshment; when done together, it allows us to recharge the spiritual batteries of our marriage.

For prayer to be effective in our relationship, we must be persistent and regular in it. Prayer does not insure that we will be insulated from the trials and tribulations that all marriages encounter, but prayer stimulates all our marriage essentials so we can remain steadfast in faith and calm in the midst of personal or marital travails. Prayer is our stimulus to grow in the face of human conflict. It is not a means of avoiding marital conflict, but a vehicle to carry us through and beyond conflict. Neither does prayer offer an escape from our marriage responsibilities; what it does offer is a magnificent means for vigorously entering into the fray of the most complicated marital predicament.

There will be times when our prayers seemingly go unanswered. The spiritual masters tells us this is because the answer might be beyond our understanding at this time in our spiritual development—we are not spiritually mature enough to be able to use the answer fruitfully. In some instances, God indeed does give us an answer, but we haven't yet developed the spiritual "eyes" to see that the prayer has indeed already been answered. All prayer is spiritual, and any answer to it must first be recognized in its spiritual form. Asking God for material things or changes may blind us to the spiritual answer that emerges.

In the context of marriage, a reason we may think that God doesn't hear our prayer is because God's answer to us is in the form of a change of attitude. Attitudinal change—actually changing our mind about the situation we have prayed about— may go completely unnoticed. A change in our own attitude may become apparent only when someone else, perhaps our spouse, inquires how we're doing regarding a life issue that previously "tied us in knots." When we respond with something like, "Oh, that doesn't bother me anymore," we are signaling how much our attitude has changed. Could this attitudinal change be God's answer to our prayer?

Notes

CHAPTER FIVE

The Fourth Marriage Essential: Intimacy

Let love be genuine; hate what is evil, hold fast to what is good; love one another with mutual affection; outdo one another in showing honor.

ROMANS 12:9-10

Evaporator	Essential	Eroder
Possessiveness	Intimacy	Indifference

Intimacy is the feeling condition created by a strong and positive emotional bond, an almost mystical bond, which produces devotion, attachment, and affection between relationship partners, and which sometimes requires personal sacrifice.

1. The Individual Level of Intimacy

Let's first identify your premier "intimacy gift." Identify *one* of the five gifts listed below as your primary gift of *intimacy,* by first studying the descriptors under each of the gifts, and then intuitively identifying which one of the five gifts is most operative in your life right now.

The five "intimacy gifts" are:

1. Joy

- expressing pleasure or delight in celebration
- showing great happiness of heart
- the unspoken, inner result of knowing that God is your true reality
- your positive emotional response to knowing that God's grace sustains you
- being jubilant or inwardly elated knowing you will have God's grace throughout your life

2. Trust

- assured reliance on God's healing power
- a mature dependence on God's love
- believing in and expecting with confidence that God's promise of abundance is being fulfilled, even now
- anticipating that all things and events will eventually turn out for the good
- consigning your life to God's care

3. Love-Finder

- feeling God's hand in everything
- awakening to God's love everywhere
- continuously discovering God's presence
- constantly detecting love in ourselves
- always recognizing God's healing power within

4. Empathy

- being emotionally "with" another
- understanding the experience of another
- becoming acutely aware of the totality of another's feelings as a profound expression of emotional intimacy
- going beyond the facts of another's experience to touch the spiritual core that is there
- walking in another's emotional "shoes"

5. *Gratitude*
- expressing profound thankfulness
- adopting a worshipful attitude toward God for giving abundant and unmerited divine assistance throughout our lives
- giving continuous praise and pious benediction to God
- adoration coupled with a sense of sanctified obligation
- recognizing the giftedness in which we live[7]

2. The Couple Level of Intimacy

Fundamentally, *intimacy* means to share. What we share in our marriages is ourselves, primarily our gifts, but also our shadows and compulsions. We need to share all of these from time to time so that we come to know more clearly who we are, and so we can help our spouse know who he or she is as well. At first, it may seem strange that we use our shadows and compulsions as teaching devices, as it were, for ourselves and our spouse. The fact is, however, that we can never genuinely and comprehensively learn our gifts—and our spouse's gifts as well—if we didn't have shadows and compulsions for comparison. The power of *intimacy* helps us more fully understand and practice our gifts by sharing ourselves fully with our spouse.

As each partner's ability for exercising intimacy increases, spouses in strong and seasoning relationships experience ever deeper understanding of one another. *Intimacy* enables each partner "to walk in the shoes of the other," which allows one partner to reflect back to the communicator what was just communicated. Such feedback demonstrates that the original

---

[7] Identify the one gift that best describes you right now, then turn to Appendix A. Your chosen gift is your "premier" individual *intimacy* gift. It is this "gift" that provides you with the primary motive power to positively and constructively address your fourth marriage essential of *intimacy*. In Appendix A, the shadow of your gift is the word to the right of your gift, and your compulsion is the word to the left of it. Appendix B contains short definitions of each of the shadows and compulsions.

communication was understood in a feeling or a factual way. Relationships that can deal with the full spectrum of feelings find a richness and a happiness unknown to others. Feelings are the movers of the drama of any marriage!

Seasoned and seasoning marriage partners who practice *intimacy* have the ability to intuitively know and attend to what the other is feeling. It's not that they are mind readers—they certainly need accurate information about the emotional feelings their partner is feeling—but once one has expressed certain feelings, an empathetic partner can immediately sense the importance of this information and is able to focus fully on the emotional twists, folds, and wrinkles that the other is experiencing. This goes far beyond "holding hands." *Intimacy* is a necessary ingredient in any marriage, and a set of skills that seasoned relationships well understand.

Partners in an intimate marriage:

- demonstrate empathy and awareness of the inner world of one another
- engage in everyday demonstrations of affection
- demonstrate a general attitude and behavioral posture of cherishing one another
- share risky feelings and deep, personal thoughts
- willingly try to help each other deal with any personal vulnerabilities (sometimes called "hot buttons")
- express genuine caring, giving, supporting, and being spontaneously helpful
- exhibit devotion and warmth to one another
- matter to each other more than anything else; they are each first on each other's list
- experience intense longing for union with one another
- experience deep communion of heart and mind
- express sexuality, body language of affirmation and celebration

- lovingly experience healthy sexual intercourse as a love act of recurrent hope
- experience passion: a burning sharing of self on all levels
- feel warm devotion toward one another
- find emotional refreshment in one another

Indifference—the Eroder of Intimacy

Indifference is:

- a sense of "it doesn't matter one way or the other"
- marked by no special like or dislike
- marked by lack of interest or concern
- apathy, mediocrity
- characterized by the lack of an active quality
- neutral, aloof, disinterested
- marked by coldness, frigidity
- unconcerned, inattentive, insensitive
- careless, neglectful, expressing no particular desire
- communicating spousal unimportance, dispassion, and a halfhearted affect
- communicating, usually without words, that one's spouse is unattractive, not valuable, and "who cares anyway?"

The Indifferent Marriage

	Compulsion	Gift	Shadow
Ellie:	Submissiveness	Gratitude	Blaming
Roy:	Ingratiation	Empathy	Obtuseness

Roy and Ellie have been married for over twenty-five years. Their two children are grown and out of the house, leaving them "empty-nesters." Ellie responded to this new style of living without the "kids" by becoming more affectively aroused. She noticed a fairly dramatic increase in her need for Roy's attention, nurturance, affection, and time. Yet whenever she approached him, he seemed to become all the more distant. Ellie's intimacy gift of gratitude was soon beginning to deteriorate into submissiveness. She found herself figuratively "tip-toeing" around Roy for fear of upsetting him. In her heart, she began blaming him for her feelings of aloneness.

Roy's reaction to the "empty-nest" was just the opposite of Ellie's—he became more independent. He reasoned that he had stepped into a new stage of life, and what he needed most was freedom. With his active fathering over, Roy dreamed of things like fishing at the lake, long drives through the countryside on his new motorcycle, Sunday afternoons of football, and evening TV entertainment. Roy's intimacy gift of empathy soon eroded into a silent obtuseness of Ellie's intimacy needs. Subliminally, he sensed that he'd been ingratiating toward Ellie's and the children's needs all through the marriage, and as a compensation Roy swung into obtuseness. He now conceives of his life in a rather singular manner. He doesn't picture Ellie with him. Roy wants solitude, aloneness, almost reclusiveness. Yet, even when he is with Ellie, over meals, at church, shopping, etc., he still doesn't seem to be genuinely present to her; he's aloof, emotionally separated, affectively someplace else.

Ellie feels alone, emotionally abandoned, and disconnected. It's as though Roy has left her. He's physically present, but psychologically absent. She feels that Roy has become indifferent to her. When Ellie looks at Roy, she only sees an "I really don't care" attitude. Ellie is more than sad, she's depressed.

Ellie's friends began to recognize the changes in her, and encouraged her to seek counseling. She worked with her counselor for several sessions before the counselor called Roy in. The three of them worked together for six or eight more sessions, defining how they could bolster their innate gifts, find new avenues of intimacy, and more directly invite God into their relationship once again. Both spouses need to rediscover their core gifts of gratitude and empathy, their primary intimacy powers.

The Indifferent/Defensive Marriage

When a sieve is shaken, the refuse appears; so do a person's
faults when he speaks.

SIRACH 27:4

Defensiveness is a state or condition of preparation for an expected aggression or attack, and/or of being devoted to resisting. In a marriage, indifference can take on a defensive posture when one spouse feels attacked or has something to hide.

Every marriage relationship travels through a period of trial and adjustment, or at least stages of shifting relationship and personal priorities. The usual pattern is that one spouse begins to feel discontent in some way. This may be coming from any of his or her life arenas. One begins to have fantasies of being single again, questions whether he or she married the "right" person, perhaps even has illusions of carving out an entirely new lifestyle. Such thoughts and daydreams are quite normal, and I'm convinced they are actually healthy because they force us to review our marriage and eventually see the goodness that is actually there. As these thoughts unfold, he or she feels a level of guilt for trying to hide this wandering imagination, which soon leads to becoming defensive. This defensiveness may take on the air of indifference as a way to create distance, both from oneself and from one's spouse whom, it is feared, may begin to inquire about the changes in behavior. In any event, while we go through such times we may appear—and to some degree actually become—defensively indifferent.

Rick and Margaret

	Compulsion	Gift	Shadow
Margaret	Hyper-euphoria	Joyfulness	Dejection
Rick:	Reductionism	Trust	Insecurity

Rick and Margaret went through such a time of defensive indifference. Rick, a successful business man, entered his mid-forties with increasingly meandering thoughts of freedom, independence, life change, and idealized love. As his thoughts intensified, his behavior toward Margaret violated most of the descriptors of intimacy. Rick's strongest gift of *intimacy* was trust, but his midlife "crisis" pushed him over into the shadow of insecurity. He was no longer sure about himself or anything else about his life. He was going through a deep review of his life, and the first stage of this review was to question almost everything. Margaret, whose gift of *intimacy* was joy, found herself slipping into the shadow of dejection. She felt Rick was pushing her away, he became "touchy," moody, and sometimes even irascible.

Finally, Margaret exploded at Rick. She rebuked his behavior and called him back to the relationship. Their communication was mostly contentious at first, but gradually they found a new respect for each other that became the catalyst for each of them to shift their intimacy gifts. Margaret began to accent "love-finder" as well as her joy, while Rick gained new appreciation for empathy, and added it to his trust. This shift, this exploration of new facets of their personalities, invigorated the overall intimacy in their marriage. Thankfully, Rick and Margaret were able to go beyond simply "weathering the storm"—they used the energy of the "storm" to grow deeper in their respect of each other and their relationship. The process took three years!

Defensiveness shows itself in a variety of ways:

- arguing in support or justification of one's "side"
- self-protective behaviors of all kinds: stone walling, warding off, holding at bay, keeping at arm's length, standing one's ground
- using defense mechanisms against one's partner: denial,

regression, repression, projection, displacement, avoidance, etc.

Other threats to *intimacy* include:

1. The work-as-worth ethic: Feeling that love must be earned through doing, achieving, producing, etc. (My personal worth is measured by the amount of work I do, both in the relationship and in other arenas of my life. If I don't work hard, then I'm not worthy of love.)
2. Affective insensitivity: Having very little vocabulary for feeling states. Inability to connect feeling states with words. Focusing on the physical or the material for fear of one's own emotions.
3. Fear of closeness: Using anger, irritability, indifference as shields to fend off emotional closeness because it's anxiety provoking.
4. Disorders of sexuality: Inappropriate psychosexual development that spawns fear of intimacy on all levels.
5. Disorders of time management and priority: Becoming overly involved, preoccupied, even compulsive about one's work or other outside activities.

The Possessive Marriage

The story of the wise man and the bird lover is appropriate here. One day, a wise man was walking in the forest when he came upon a bird lover. This man truly loved birds—he wanted to be around them always. It seemed to him that if he wasn't around birds his life simply wasn't whole. In his desperation, the man set a trap for birds. When he captured one he would grasp it tightly in his hand. All the while, the bird would squirm and squeal in an attempt to free itself from the man's heavy grip. Naturally, every time the man would loosen his grip to view the beauty of the bird, the bird would simply fly away.

The man really didn't enjoy this practice, but he didn't know what else to do. The wise man made a simple suggestion. "If you put a few seeds in your open hand, the birds will eventually fly to you and eat out of your hand."

We can become possessive of our spouse because of our need for attention, affection, and love. Possessiveness may be a response to a deep-seated fear of losing our spouse. To remedy this insecure situation, we can enter into a paradoxical behavior of trying to insure that he or she stays close at hand by becoming possessive. Possessiveness is characterized by attempts to dominate, control, manipulate, and otherwise influence our spouse.

Connie and Max

	Compulsion	Gift	Shadow
Connie:	Pollyannaism	Love-finder	Fault-seeker
Max:	Hyper-euphoria	Trust	Insecurity

Connie and Max had a possessive relationship. They had married very young; they were high school sweethearts. Max was the star of the football team and Connie was the lead cheerleader. Max loved Connie very much, but was afraid of his dependency on her. Deep down, Max didn't know how he would ever survive without Connie. In addition, his jealously seemed to have no bounds. Max's conception of himself as the robust, hyper-masculine, steer-you-own-course kind of guy clashed with his hidden dependence on Connie. The way he worked out his dilemma was to become possessive. His gift of trust was decidedly eroded by his shadow of insecurity. He tried to dominate his own insecurity by holding on to Connie as tight as he knew how. Naturally, intimacy was crushed. Connie's gift of love-finder had never truly developed, and she was still deluding herself in a pollyannaism which forced her to see everything as "wonderful."

In the early stages of the marriage, Connie interpreted Max's behavior simply as his way of showing her his loving attention. As she grew emotionally, she began to realize that her relationship with Max was lacking something. Eventually, this pushed her toward the shadow of fault-seeker, which she directed at Max. This was where turmoil and confusion, fighting and arguing, broke out in Connie's and Max's marriage.

Eventually, Connie and Max were able to grow. They found spiritual and relational support, not to mention new intimacy building skills in *Marriage Encounter*. It was a lifesaver for their marriage. Max learned that Connie could return his love so much better if he only changed his grasping, heavy-gripping behaviors to more respectful loving ones. Max was able to truly find his gift of trust. Once this happened, and once Connie could give up her pollyannaish ways and really "own" her gift of love-finder, the intimacy in the marriage soared.

3. The Spiritual Level of Intimacy

For God did not call us to impurity but in holiness.
Therefore whoever rejects this rejects not human authority but
God, who also gives his Holy Spirit to you.

1 Thessalonians 4:7-8

Holy Groundedness

When the essential condition of *intimacy* grows sufficiently in a relationship, this facilitates the birth of "holy groundedness." This is the spiritual relationship condition in a marriage where each partner feels a sense of couple stability coming from a deeply seated sharing between the couple and God, i.e., they feel their marriage is holy ground.

Holy groundedness is deep spiritual intimacy. *Intimacy* means sharing, and spiritual intimacy involves sharing your spirit freely with your partner. Spiritual intimacy propels each partner to act as a spiritual font of refreshment for the other. Each is the spiritual well where the other goes to quench any spiritual thirst and, in the process, restores to the other a renewed sense of who he/she is. Each partner spiritually "grounds" the other by reminding him or her of his/her being and call.

Spiritual intimacy on a couple level is attained at ever deeper levels when each partner takes an active role in helping the other capture, identify, embrace, understand, and express his or her unique spiritual personality in everyday living. When each partner assumes this role of honoring and cherishing the spiritual personality power inherent in the other, a new level of *intimacy* is experienced—the relationship is holy ground, a grand miracle sculpted by God uniquely as the path of redemption for both. Each partner is spiritually grounded in the other, and together they form a grounding where they find freedom to explore and express their unique, true, and spiritual selves. This is an intimacy where both delight in each other, find joy in their interactions, and daily choose one another. The love of Jesus is reflected in the love that marriage partners give to one another. Holy groundedness means that we are called by God to always remember, even put first, the feelings and desires of our spouse.

Sex is part of spiritual intimacy, and we feel our partner's love through our sharing of our bodies as well. In our sexual behavior, we walk the holy ground of life knowing that God has blessed this intimate physical sharing, has made it pleasurable as a kind of glimpse or foretaste of the immense pleasure of the truth, beauty, and goodness in being united with God. Sex is a sharing of self unlike any other; it needs to be intimate, a deep sharing in the full sense of the word, and not simply private or secretive. Sex grounded in holiness gives us an identifiably different and deeper relationship with our spouse than we could possibly share with anyone else. This sexual intimacy touches the sacred place of honor within us where God resides.

The wedding ceremony is more than a nice social occasion— it's a holy vocation and an invitation to live on holy ground. It is an inauguration of a journey of holiness directed by love. It is only in giving our selves away that we can begin the process of growing toward holiness together. This holy intimacy elevates our sharing to a higher priority than even our most staunchly held convictions. *Intimacy* involves a purpose bigger than any thought we could entertain.

The more affectionate the intimacy, the higher the quality of the relationship. *Intimacy* is always tender, compassionate, gentle, and kind—never coarse, sharp, rough, or neglectful. It provides us with a sustained understanding that our spouse truly does care for us. Holy groundedness calls for a completely open involvement with our spouse. There is nothing partial, selective, or closed about intimacy rooted in holy groundedness. True and holy intimacy lets our spouse into the secrets of our desires, trials, joys, fears...everything. Our spouse is our first and foremost confidant/e.

Notes

CHAPTER SIX

The Fifth Marriage Essential: Trust

Welcome one another, therefore, just as Christ has welcomed you, for the glory of God.

ROMANS 15:7

Evaporator	Essential	Eroder
Blind Faith	Trust	Doubt

Trust is the couple level relationship condition created when each partner can rely upon the other without question; when each genuinely accepts the other unconditionally; and when each partner willingly anticipates, expects, and facilitates the growth and development of the other as a human being of dynamic worth.

1. The Individual Level of Trust

Before exploring the fifth marriage essential, that of *trust*, first identify your premier "trust gift." Identify *one* of the five gifts listed on the following pages as your primary gift of *trust* by first studying the descriptors under each of the gifts, and then intuitively identifying which one of the five gifts is most operative in your life right now.

The five "trust gifts" are:

1. *Harmony*
- when all parts are in accordance with a central principle
- many pieces existing in a unified calmness and constituting a consistent whole
- being "in sync" with the will of God
- being in concurrence with the central principle of God's love
- living in symmetry with God, i.e., in alignment with peace

2 *Patience*
- tapping into the mysterious calm in the universe
- calmly continuing in the face of adversity or hardship
- transcending worldly impulses, replacing them with God's love
- transforming irritability and annoyance into peace
- replacing the frantic excitement of the world with God's illuminating light

3. *Strength*
- the potency and ability to accomplish things
- the tough ability to resist attack of any kind
- knowing that one cannot be spiritually hurt in any way
- being straightforward and upright in action
- having the capacity for sustained exertion

4. *Transcendence*
- to go beyond the physical plane into another dimension of being
- flowing from the worldly level to the spiritual level
- transforming oneself to a new paradigm
- being fundamentally changed, converted, dramatically altered
- a "sea change" or core shift to what is truly real

5. Self-Discipline
- enforcing obedience from one part of yourself onto another
- molding one's own character in accordance with learned principles, values, or precepts
- imposing order upon yourself
- placing supremacy of spiritual self as one's primary goal
- developing in ways unattainable before[8]

Trust is a felt sense of an assured reliance on someone or something, knowing the other is "there" for you. Wherever you place your *trust*, is where your faith rests as well. *Trust* gives us the power to grow through adversity. *Trust* offers peace in knowing that all will be well. *Trust* engenders hope that God's will be done, that you are part of God's plan, and that God will not let you down in the people and the abundance that is brought your way. *Trust* opens our eyes to reliability, so that we can depend upon one another. Confidence is the fruit of *trust*.

2. The Couple Level of Trust

In a marriage, *trust* teaches responsibility, permanence, and stability. It makes the relationship a place of solid belief and security, confidence and strength, and of conviction and unity. *Trust* empowers us to place ourselves in the hands of another and gives us permission to take risks that otherwise wouldn't be possible. *Trust* allows us to let go of trying to control and dominate everything. By "letting things be," we can leave

---

[8] Identify the one gift that best describes you right now, then turn to Appendix A. Your chosen gift is your "premier" individual *trust* gift. It is this "gift" that provides you with the primary motive power to positively and constructively address your third marriage essential of *trust* In Appendix A, the shadow of your gift is the word to the right of your gift, and your compulsion is the word to the left of it. Appendix B contains short definitions of each of the shadows and compulsions.

behind always "doing" things and get on with the "being" of our lives. *Trust* assumes reliability, credibility, and anticipation of good things to come. We consign our *trust* to our spouse when we marry. If and when this *trust* is damaged, the hurt is palpable and deep, the recuperation time is wearisome, and healing is impossible without God.

The couple relationship condition of *trust* includes:

- demonstrating a true acceptance of the ongoing process of individuation
- allowing and helping each other to grow and develop fully, into all that we can be
- allowing and even fostering positive change
- practicing forgiveness of faults
- being considerately honest rather than being brutally frank
- exhibiting personal reliability at our core
- honoring "being there" for one another every day, and especially during life stage transitions
- encouraging faith, reliance, belief in, expectation of good, and confidence in one another
- relying upon, depending upon, and counting on one another
- being responsible, believable, constant, true, and loyal
- being able to truly "deliver" to and for one another
- relying on the truthfulness or accuracy of one's spouse; believing in one another
- giving credit to one another
- a charge or duty imposed in faith or confidence or as a condition of the marriage relationship
- something entrusted to one to be used or carried out in the interest of another

Acceptance—a Central Component of Trust

Acceptance is part of *trust*. Acceptance in a marriage does not mean submissiveness, nor does it mean resignation. Quite the contrary, acceptance helps you to see things as they truly are in reality. According to *Webster*, acceptance means to regard as proper, normal, and inevitable, and to undertake the responsibility for. Acceptance means to be approving, honoring, and assenting—having a sense of being in accord with another. In marriage, acceptance instills a graciousness of heart and allows you to radiate your own giftedness outward, all the while recognizing the truth, beauty, and goodness of your spouse. Acceptance allows you to give permission to your spouse to be different from who and what you are. Acceptance opens you up to the valuable trust that exists in all of God's children.

The opposite of acceptance is dissension, always fighting for your own self and your perceived "rights." Dissension leads to close-mindedness and hardheartedness, neither of which gives a firm foundation for any enduring relationship with another. This quality of acceptance enables you to become inclined to enter into a contract as an equal partner, rather than with a superior attitude.

Acceptance includes:

- adaptability to change, and acceptance of individuation
- each partner facilitating one another's personal, emotional, social, intellectual, psychological, and spiritual growth
- forgiveness of faults
- accommodating the "new" me and the "new" you
- generative cooperation, and offering approval
- "educating" each other
- becoming mirrors of and for each other

- fulfilling each spouse's need for exclusivity
- being considerately honest vs. being frank

The Accepting Marriage

	Compulsion	Gift	Shadow
Reno:	Indecision	Harmony	Chaos
Rob:	Unreality	Transcendence	Worldliness

Reno and Rob faced each other in tears. Rob had just confessed that over the past four months he had involved himself in an extramarital affair. Reno was dumbfounded and speechless. Conflicting emotions cascaded over her like water over Niagara Falls. All she could do was ask, "Why? Why? Why?", but Rob had no answer. All he could say was to repeat over and over, "I don't know! I'm so sorry." Their conversation that first evening simply ripped open the wound—healing was far off. Reno didn't sleep that night, her mind reeled with inquiries about herself, about Rob, about her marriage, and about her faith. Rob, on the other hand, had the best night's sleep he'd had in a long time. His secret was out, he had confessed; he felt some relief. Yet he too experienced a deep pain knowing that Reno, his beloved wife, was suffering.

For the first time in her marriage, Reno moved into doubt. Her couple level "trust gift" of *harmony* dissolved into her shadow of chaos. She felt "out of sync" with everything and everyone; her world had collapsed, and she didn't know what to do; she had no more peace, only fragmentation and brokenness. As her chaos inflated, some of her other shadows emerged: rigidity, fear, and—most of all—blaming. Reno latched upon blaming, and gave it full vent. Reno was the woman scorned, and her anger knew no boundaries. She ranted and raved at Rob for betraying her trust. "Now, I'm left with nothing!" she bellowed. Her rage was punctuated with long periods of silence, a disconcerted reverie where she would emotionally go far away. She felt like she couldn't share this terrible news with anyone, and held on to her secret with a brewing vengeance.

Through it all, Rob held on to faith, perhaps blind faith. He was emotionally confused and his thinking was muddled. His compulsion of unreality had pulled him into the affair. Now he was still in unreality, although of a different kind; he presumed that their marriage would now simply return to where it was before the affair. In his mind, the affair was over, and as much as he tried to have empathy for Reno, he truly thought that she should let it go too. His behavioral consequence was blind faith. He never tired of exclaiming to Reno, "Don't worry, everything will be all right." His rationale was that he had learned his lesson and had no intention of returning to the affair or any other marital transgression. For Reno, the possibility of Rob's returning to the affair was not the issue. Her shadow of chaos now was translated to her compulsion of indecision. For her, the central issue was the loss of trust. Would she ever be able to regain it, and how could she live in a marriage without it?

After a month of marital standoff, Reno and Rob reconstituted their relationship enough to agree on seeing a counselor. The counselor was able to plumb Rob's emotions and begin to assemble some semblance of why this had happened in his life. Rob was kind, he didn't defend himself in some illusionary blame against Reno. He was upright and straightforward with himself; he owned up to his sin. He asked for forgiveness and was willing to make amends.

Gradually, Reno's frozen feelings began to thaw; she began to entertain at least the possibility that trust could enter into the marriage again. The warmth of acceptance was beginning to dawn in her life. In her deep contemplation, she analyzed her pre-affair relationship with Rob and was able to see some elements that needed changing. She could accept this also. She hadn't caused Rob's affair, and it was not her responsibility, but she could accept that she was party to the reconciliation that needed to grow in their relationship if her marriage with Rob was to find solid ground once again.

Doubt—the Eroder of Trust

Jesus immediately reached out his hand and caught him, saying to him, "You of little faith, why did you doubt?"

MATTHEW 14:31

Doubt is:

- lacking in confidence, being uncertain
- being fearful
- being uncertain of belief which interferes with decision-making
- hesitating in thought and action
- an inclination not to believe or trust
- leaving something open to question
- lacking conviction
- being decidedly undecided
- raising questions about worth, honesty, or validity
- being dubious: equivocal, unsettled, undecided, questionable
- becoming unreliable on many planes

The Doubting Marriage

	Compulsion	Gift	Shadow
Renatta:	Brutishness	Strength	Impotence
Juan:	Unresponsiveness	Patience	Impulsion

Renatta and Juan lived with their two sons and three daughters in a house they had just purchased on the other side of town. They had moved there at Renatta's request. She was becoming increasingly suspicious of a growing relationship between Juan and a woman in the neighborhood. This woman had lost her husband two years before in an auto accident, and since then Juan was spending time at her house helping her. At first, Renatta was pleased that Juan had taken a "Good Samaritan" interest in her, and she felt empathy toward her, realizing what losing Juan would mean. Over time, however, she became suspicious that Juan interests weren't completely altruistic. Juan seemed to talk about her, seemed eager to get over to her house to fix this or that, or to carry something heavy from the basement to the backyard.

After three months of this, Renatta inquired if Juan anticipated spending quite so much time over at the neighbor's house as he had been. "Isn't it time to let her work things out more independently?" she asked. Juan blew up. "How can you be so cold toward her?" he ranted. "How can you be comfortable just abandoning her?" he demanded. The intensity of his response intuitively told Renatta that her suspicion may be accurate. If something hadn't already happened between them, it wasn't far off. That's when Renatta requested that they move. Juan and she had talked about moving before the neighbor's husband was killed, but the issue seemed to be dropped after his death. Renatta pushed hard for the move. Reluctantly, Juan agreed and even though it took longer than she had expected, the move was finally accomplished. Renatta felt relieved that Juan was out of temptation.

Several weeks after the move, however, she was shocked when Juan came home without his wedding ring on his finger. When she asked about it, Juan defensively stated that he was doing some heavy work and didn't want to damage the ring; it was in his pocket. "Could it be that Juan is still seeing the neighbor lady?" wondered Renatta. Doubt and emotional insecurity swirled around her. She didn't know what to do, where to turn, how to proceed.

Juan's usual gift of patience was distorted into impulsiveness as he entered what could only be called an emotional affair with the widow. Consequently, he became unresponsive to Renatta. Renatta was blessed with the power of strength. When she had first noticed her husband's growing unresponsiveness, she fearfully entered her shadow of impotence. Since she didn't know what to do with her gathering doubt, she did nothing. It was not until Juan's absentmindedness with his ring that she quickly moved back into her strength. Renatta successfully resisted moving into her compulsion of brutishness, which happens so often in situations like this. (When "rejected" spouses want to retaliate against the "offending" spouse by doing something shocking like developing an extramarital relationship—supposedly to "make their spouse jealous." Actions like this are brutish and seldom helpful.)

Renatta consulted a counselor, who advised her that her feelings were real and that she needed to take some action. He advised that she confront Juan with her suspicions and ask him directly, "Is anything going on between you and the widow?" Hopefully, Juan would come in to join them in counseling.

The Blind Faith Marriage

	Compulsion	Gift	Shadow
Lana:	Brutishness	Strength	Impotence
Mike	Self-repression	Self-discipline	Self-indulgent

Lana reached for the sugar bowl. Her tea was already cold, but her emotions were red hot. Her husband Mike had just been admitted to the hospital for the third time in six months. His diagnosis: depression. Their twenty-seven years of marriage had entered a new phase four years ago when the company that Mike had founded, only three years prior, had collapsed in financial ruin. Lana had been against the formation of the company from the beginning, but those were the days, she reminisced, when she blindly accepted anything that came from Mike. Now the tables had turned. Unable to personally integrate his business failure, Mike had retreated into illness and helplessness. At first, he did seem to have legitimate medical issues that needed care; but once these few were remedied, he couldn't seem to gather enough emotional energy to reenter the labor force. He seemed broken, lifeless, directionless, and spiritually anemic. Lana found herself doubting not only the diagnosis of depression but everything about Mike—most of all, the authenticity of their marriage.

Lana berated herself for being so foolish the first twenty years of their marriage, when she was caught in her shadow of impotence and blindly consented to whatever Mike wanted. It certainly hadn't been a marriage between equals. Mike seemed so strong, so self-disciplined and self-directed. Lana had never been blessed with this type of direction, and she was in awe of his knowledge of the world, whereas she always felt so naive. Now she reasoned that Mike had entered some level of unreality, some unfocused and self-indulgent place that pushed her beyond whatever patience she possessed. Lana became unresponsive to his needs. She felt duped, tricked, betrayed by her own husband. Lana realized that she had formerly been caught in a blind faith of Mike, and that now she had moved completely over to doubt. Would he emotionally recover? Would she be able to show him any love at all? Would their marriage survive? Did she have any strength left to devote to the marriage?

Mike seemed to have no patience with Lana either, and seemed incapable of generating any empathy for what she was experiencing. Self-absorbed in his own needs, he blamed her for not being more caring and compassionate of his situation. Mike wanted care and attention, but Lana could only think that he wanted to be taken care of. She couldn't find the means to help Mike. Perhaps, she reasoned, she was simply undecided about the future of the marriage. The turmoil she felt was intense, and the future didn't look hopeful. Would she ever find a way to trust herself? Would she ever find a way to trust her husband? Would she find trust again in her marriage, if, in fact, she had ever possessed it?

Fearing being exploited and let down again, Lana grew ever more suspicious, mistrustful, and skeptical. She felt that Mike had betrayed her and dominated her all along. What was she to do now? Slowly, she discovered her own gift of strength. She came to realize her own potency, and understood that this strength had been with her all along, but that she had been too indecisive to let it come out. With Mike having been all too willing to take up the slack and make the decisions, Lana had let her gifts lay fallow. It was now time to assert herself, to place her trust in God and come to own her full sense of self. Here was the salvation for this marriage. Lana needed to forgive herself, forgive Mike, and come to own her true, real self in a way that she never had before.

3. The Spiritual Level of Trust

Put away from you all bitterness and wrath and anger and wrangling and slander, together with all malice, and be kind to one another, tenderhearted, forgiving one another, as God in Christ has forgiven you.

EPHESIANS 4:31-32

Redeeming Forgiveness

"Redeeming forgiveness" is the spiritual relationship condition created in a marriage when each partner chooses to let God's healing absolution permeate the both of them. When the condition of *trust* pervades the couple level of the marriage, its presence automatically facilitates the birth of redeeming forgiveness on the spiritual level.

Forgiveness does not mean forgetting, excusing, or even pardoning. At its center, forgiveness means that we give up whatever claim to recompense we may have thought we were due because of an injustice that was perpetrated against us. Jesus calls us to go far beyond "an eye for an eye and a tooth for a tooth." Jesus brought us the good news that forgiveness is our path to happiness. Without a forgiving heart, most relationships would rather quickly disintegrate into dispassionate distance, withdrawal, and avoidance. Seasoned and seasoning relationships have found that the bridge to happiness and longevity in the relationship is built with forgiveness, forgiveness, and more forgiveness.

Forgiveness is a gift from God that restores the innate qualities of truth, beauty, and goodness which reside in us all. These truths have been clouded over by acts or omissions so offensive that one spouse may become blind to the inner worth of the "offender." Forgiveness returns this worth to its rightful place. Forgiveness entails a shift in our internal power. When one spouse sees him or herself as victimized or hurt by the other, all perception, thinking, and feeling is so colored by this fact that it eventually overshadows the ability to see any gifts in oneself or in one's spouse. Forgiveness, however, can be more powerful than the hurt; when forgiveness arrives, it gradually forces out the lesser power of the hurt.

Forgiveness means deciding to give up resentment. Forgiveness means blessing your spouse and recognizing the offense as a personal lesson in love. Forgiveness means that we are choosing to replace the current turmoil of anger with the mighty gift of relationship peace—we are replacing the separation with the six essentials of a healthy, happy, and holy marriage. Forgiveness is the act of letting go. We must distinguish between the act of forgiving and the feeling of forgiveness.

The beginning of the act of forgiveness comes when we adopt a simple willingness to let go the tyranny of

perceiving our spouse as somehow evil. Once such willingness forms in our soul, the grace of God slowly begins seeping into our very core, and the relationship begins experiencing the emotional sweetness of forgiveness. Both spouses
begin to feel freedom from the oppressive internal torment that
had confounded and bedeviled each of them.

So often we want retribution, a payback, or at least restitu-
tion from our spouse before we begin the process of forgiveness. We want more than amends—we want the other to hurt
as much, or more, than we did. Yet forgiveness is quite different from the selfish encumbrances we place on it. We put the
cart before the "horse of forgiveness," as it were, when we
think that we need to *feel* forgiveness before we can begin the
act of forgiveness. Forgiveness begins with a decision that forgiveness is what we do in a Christian marriage—this is what
distinguishes a Christian marriage. Without the decision to
begin the act of forgiveness, the relief that forgiveness offers
will never emerge. We need to enter into the act of forgiveness
before our distorted feelings can start healing—it is the pre-
requisite for our broken feelings gradually being replaced by
feelings of peace and the relationship returned to its gifted
harmony through reconciliation.

What Forgiveness Is Not

Forgiveness is hard for us; at our primal core, it is perceived
as contrary to our natural instincts. We seem much more comfortable with the notion of "an eye for an eye...". When trying
to understand a concept, it is sometimes helpful to look at its
opposite—that which it is not. This is particularly true with
forgiveness, because we may confuse true forgiveness with other
actions that bear little resemblance to it. Forgiveness is not
repressing our grudges, nor is it pretending everything is just
fine.

Forgiveness does not mean hiding our anger from the

"offending spouse" by placing our wrath on inanimate objects, or projecting it on to other people. Kicking the dog, slamming your fist on the table, yelling at the kids, or using expletives at all the drivers around you, have nothing to do with forgiveness. While forgiveness is our goal, we must be assertive enough to directly and forthrightly bring our partner to task over his or her behavior. We must let our spouse know how his or her action hurt us. The offense must be cleanly exposed and clearly delineated, as a requisite part of the forgiveness process.

Another, more commonly misplaced notion of forgiveness is that it is a condescending pardon of the "offending spouse," done in a benevolent way, which somehow earns or entitles the "forgiving spouse" some strange moral superiority over the offender. Forgiveness means that we cease to think that the offender is bad, and regain a more centered thinking that our spouse is simply another child of God. This helps us give up any unhelpful thinking that separates us from the love that resides within our God-given love partner. When we decide to forgive, it is not some circuitous admission that we ourselves are somehow wrong. Some spouses mistakenly think that one or the other must be wrong, so if I forgive my spouse, that somehow makes me the offending party. Such convoluted thinking only muddies the water and prevents us from entering the process of forgiveness.

Forgiveness does not mean we are making an excuse for the other—that what he or she did is now somehow all right. Forgiveness does not absolve the offender from responsibility for his or her action, nor does it relinquish any accountability for the consequences of his or her offense. What was done is still wrong, but in forgiveness we choose to focus on the love that resides in the heart of our loved one more than on the offense. Forgiveness does not *require* the offending spouse to claim remorse, or even to make amends. Forgiveness comes with no strings attached, no demands for apologies. We forgive without the guarantee that our offending spouse will do anything to "set the record straight" in any way.

CHAPTER SEVEN

The Sixth Marriage Essential: Commitment

May the God of steadfastness and encouragement grant you to live in harmony with one another, in accordance with Christ Jesus, so that together you may with one voice glorify the God and Father of our Lord Jesus Christ.

ROMANS 15:5-6

Evaporator	Essential	Eroder
Codependence	Commitment	Avoidance

Commitment is the human relationship condition created when each partner exercises personal perseverance, patience, and stamina so that fidelity and courageous steadfastness can grow strong over a lifetime.

1. The Individual Level of Commitment

Identify *one* of the five gifts listed on the following pages as your premier "commitment gift" by first studying the descriptors under each of the gifts, and then intuitively identifying which one of the five gifts is most operative in your life right now. This is not to say that all gifts are in some ways functioning in your life, but generally one of them emerges as the most potent, all other things being equal.

The five "commitment gifts" are:

1. Honesty/Truth
- being fair, sincere, and true to the primary fact of God
- having elevated honor and integrity
- freedom from internal fraud and deception
- letting the petty and/or the trivial go so it doesn't clutter your life
- going beyond mere worldly honesty and entering into emotional and even spiritual honesty

2. Inspiration
- to be infused with light and life
- to be motivated by the brilliance of the celestial reality
- to touch the spiritual reality within you
- to acknowledge the mighty mechanisms of care and cure deep within you
- to recognize God's healing power and strength working wonders in your life

3. Kindness
- demonstrating gentle, affectionate, and loving behavior
- accepting your body as a gift from God
- being tender, mild, friendly, and helpful
- giving care
- acting with courteous gesture and goodwill

4. Steadfastness
- being fixed in place, immovable
- being firm in belief, determined, loyal, and adherent
- being sure of movement, unfaltering
- having the qualities of constancy, purposefulness, dependability, and steadiness
- being staunch, resolute, and principled

5. Perseverance
- persistently plodding in your cause, mission, or ministry
- having singleness of purpose, tenacity
- proceeding when others would have lost hope
- running the extra mile, the extra mile, and the extra mile—having stamina, backbone, courage, and spiritual grit
- staying focused on the light of God even when your spiritual upper room is dark[9]

2. The Couple Level of Commitment

Let endurance have its full effect, so that you may be mature and complete, lacking in nothing.

JAMES 1:4

The Dynamics of Commitment

Commitment, or staying power, is a gift from God which gives you the strength to persistently carry on in your cause, your mission, and in your vocation of marriage. For seasoned and seasoning marriage partners, the mission—the ministry—is the health and growth of the marriage. *Commitment* means having singleness of purpose and tenacity. *Commitment* means proceeding when others may have lost hope, running the extra mile, having stamina, backbone, courage, and spiritual grit. Every one of these qualities performs a crucial role in relationships that continue over the long term.

How are we called to exercise this aspect of marital *commitment*? Marriage is a covenant between two of God's

---

[9] Now turn to Appendix A. The one gift you have chosen here is considered your premier gift of *commitment*. It is this "gift" (in Appendix A) that provides you with the primary motive, positively and constructively, to address your couple essential of *commitment*. As you did in the previous chapter, in Appendix A identify the shadow of your gift, (the word to the right of your gift), and your compulsion (the word to the left of your gift). You may want to consult the definitions of the shadows and compulsions in Appendix B.

children, a sacred union of two people intent on seeking to live together in the blessedness of God's care. Anything that brings us closer to God is blessed. How can we see the union that binds us, our own marriage, as blessed? If not blessed, then what?

To be sure, there are times when all relationships fall out of romantic love; the love is still there, but something has covered it over. The spouses still feel love *for* each other, but they may not feel *in* love with each other. This "falling in and out of love" happens many times over the course of any marriage; it's normal and natural, if also somewhat scary. The quality of commitment carries the marriage through such times of confusion, gives emotional stability, offers a vision of the future, and a sense that "this too shall pass" throughout the marital relationship challenge.

Committed marriages:

- actively sustain aspects of loving
- work toward developing balance in the relationship
- consistently focus on marital continuity and predictability
- facilitate personal growth in both spouses
- are mutually supportive, especially during critical moments of change, i.e., crises of addition and crises of attrition
- see the couple partnership as "till death do us part"
- celebrate family ties on both sides of the marriage
- feel that unswerving connection exists in their marriage
- build a sustaining friendship between spouses that continues over the long haul
- consciously inject the qualities of perseverance, tenacity, and stamina in their marriage
- establish and maintain positive couple habits, traditions, and rituals
- honor relationship history
- practice steadiness, wanting to be *at* and *on* each other's side

Avoidance—the Primary Eroder of Commitment

But fornication and impurity of any kind, or greed, must not even be mentioned among you, as is proper among saints. Entirely out of place is obscene, silly, and vulgar talk; but instead, let there be thanksgiving.

EPHESIANS 5:3-4

We all prefer to avoid things we don't like. We can find ingenious ways of dodging something taxing or someone we consider noxious or threatening. Avoidance is no stranger to some marriages. When we are ashamed of what we have done or what we have neglected in our marriages, we try to somehow slide around the topic—we avoid. When we feel rejected, we often retreat—we avoid. When we feel inadequate, weak, confused, or depressed, we find ways of escaping—we avoid. How do you avoid your spouse at times?

We avoid when we:

- evade, dodge, or parry
- elude, flee, or retreat
- recoil, recede from, or depart
- escape, circumvent, shun, steer away, shy away, or keep away
- steer clear of, give a wide berth, shirk, or malinger

The Avoiding Marriage

	Compulsion	Gift	Shadow
Linda:	Excitability	Inspiration	Deadened
Gene:	Codependency	Kindness	Indifference

Gene and Linda were married only two years, and they were already in my counseling office! They began their story with their dating behavior. From Gene's standpoint, Linda had pursued him. Not that he minded. Linda was beautiful, bright, and articulate—all the characteristics that a young man dreams of in a wife. Linda admitted that this was true. She fell in love with Gene for all the reasons that one would think: Gene was handsome, ambitious, adventuresome, socially adept, and attentive to her. More than all this, however, Linda fell in love with Gene's family. Her family was fragmented and chaotic; his, on the other hand, was warm, accepting, loving, compassionate, and most of all, a unit. Linda longed for this sense of family in her life.

In the first year of the marriage, Linda moved directly to her compulsion of excitability. Linda was excited, she was thrilled that she had found Gene and his family. She would go to work every day and return to prepare gourmet meals, she would groom and primp herself to look her very best, even at the breakfast table. Linda would singlehandedly keep their apartment looking like a show place. She had to make everything "just right." Her physical and sexual attentiveness to Gene became overzealous.

Through all this, Gene was going in the opposite psychological direction. Gene's gift of kindness was fast eroding into indifference. He became more and more emotionally unavailable, more presumptuous of Linda's care, more blind to his part in the marriage. In a very curious way, Gene combined his compulsion and his shadow, becoming indifferently codependent on Linda's compulsion of excitability. For one full year, Linda willingly carried this burden, but eventually cracks appeared in her armor. The energy of her excitability was seeping out, and she gradually felt her shadow of emotional deadness become stronger as she sensed the balance in the marriage slipping. That's when she started her avoidance behaviors. She would stay late at work, and when she did get home she said she wasn't hungry. Formerly a sparkling conversationalist, she became all but mute toward Gene. The apartment was left unattended, the bills unpaid, and the laundry discarded in piles. Where she had formerly taken on all this work gladly, almost demanding it, offering all her work in service to the marriage, she now had taken a complete turnaround and became utterly deadened to the marriage. Gene tried in vain to pick up the slack he had formerly left to Linda, but the damage had been done. Finally, her avoidance escalated into a silence precluding any communication. With each of the six marriage essentials damaged and repair blocked by extreme avoidance, there remained little to retrieve. Eventually, Linda simply moved out.

Withdrawal—Another Eroder of Commitment

Withdrawal is a cousin of avoidance, yet somewhat different in behavioral style. We generally think of avoidance as behavior we engage in while we are with our spouse; withdrawal, as it is described here, means physically removing yourself from your spouse's presence.

We withdraw when we:

- retreat, retire, or elude
- depart, absent ourselves, or relinquish
- keep aloof, keep apart, seclude ourselves
- extract ourselves, become unsociable, and/or nongregarious

The Withdrawn Marriage

	Compulsion	Gift	Shadow
Amy:	Imperiousness	Perseverance	Resignation
Nick:	Skepticism	Truth	Deceit

Amy and Nick had several grown children, and six grandchildren. Nick had taken retirement five years ago. By personality type, Amy was an introvert, and as she matured, she became increasing so. Amy had always cherished and protected her private time. She would take herself to a movie and frequent museums alone. She liked long solitary walks, and she made frequent visits to her church for meditative prayer. This was just "who she was." Amy wasn't running away from anyone or anything, she was simply acting out her personality, which made her prefer to be alone perhaps more than others did.

Nick's retirement became a challenge for Amy. As a gratified accountant who spent lots of time in his office, Nick had not spent much time around the house. When he retired, this changed completely. Nick's constant presence unnerved Amy— she felt conflicted, out of sorts, dejected, despondent, and insecure. On the one hand, she knew that she loved Nick and felt that she should want to be with him. On the other hand, she craved her private time. Without it, she began to unravel. Nick seemed obtuse to Amy's plight. As a private person, Amy kept most of her thoughts and feelings inside of herself, and this dilemma was no different. Amy's gift was perseverance; she could plod through almost anything, but Nick's presence in the house all day long pushed her over to her shadow of giving up. The way she chose to give up was to withdraw from Nick as much as she could.

Amy began taking longer outings. She went to the mall more and more, and even started taking her evening meal out. She visited her sister in Florida three times in six months, where she loved to simply walk the beach. She withdrew from Nick in any and every way possible. Nick was confused. His idea of retirement had been to spend lots of time with Amy, taking trips, golfing, socializing with friends, and perhaps even taking classes together. None of Nick's retirement dreams were being realized. His gift of *truth,* which formerly energized his commitment with a burning fervor of attachment to Amy, their home, and family was gradually slipping into his compulsion of skepticism. "Maybe she isn't the right woman for me after all!" he mused. "Perhaps she hasn't been from the beginning. I've probably just been deceiving myself all these years, thinking I was happy. When I really see how she is, I don't feel loved at all," he thought. Fragmented and feeling victimized, Nick didn't know which way to turn.

Codependency—the Evaporator of Commitment

So much has been said and written about codependency, and the term has been applied so liberally to so many behaviors, that its definition seems to have lost clarity. Codependency refers to a life condition where one spouse becomes so over-involved in his or her spouse's own dependency (whether this dependency be alcoholism, workaholism, drug addiction, gambling, chronic sickness, or other chronically unhealthy behavior patterns) that the nonaddicted spouse becomes dependent on his or her spouse's dependency, hence becoming codependent. Codependency is a state of overcommitment, where one spouse is all but mesmerized by something going on in the other spouse's life, to such an unhealthy degree that the first spouse loses control of his or her own life.

The classic example of the codependent relationship is the wife who becomes so consumed with her husband's alcoholism that she herself becomes addicted to her husband's addicted behavior. She tries everything she can to help him, while at the same time heroically hiding it from neighbors, family, supervisors, and the like. It's not that she can't (or wouldn't like to) do without her husband's alcoholism, it's just that her own thoughts have become addicted to thinking about her husband's addiction, in a manner similar to the way her husband's thoughts are addicted to alcohol. Over time, as he doesn't know how to live without alcohol, she likewise "forgets" how to live without her thoughts and behavioral addiction to her husband's addiction. I know this seems convoluted, yet codependency is not at all rare. Indeed, it is rather common.

Real and true *commitment* evaporates under the strain of codependency. Rather than a *commitment*, codependency means:

- giving over your entire self in service to the unhealthy dependence of your spouse
- "protecting" the unrealistic "wants" of your spouse who is in some way ill
- allowing your spouse's unhealthy needs and wants to dominate your own life
- feeling compelled to assist your spouse's flaws or addicted behavior
- having no limits on the amount of service you will render your spouse's unhealthy desires

The Codependent Marriage

	Compulsion	Gift	Shadow
Barbara:	Codependency	Kindness	Indifference
Al:	Fixation	Steadfast	Unreliable

Barbara and Al have been married for well over thirty years. In the first years, Al was a functional alcoholic, in that he abused alcohol not to the point where he couldn't work, yet certainly to the degree that his drinking had a very negative impact on the marriage. This is where Barbara's codependency began. She worried intensely about her husband, and especially about his drinking. All day long, she would fret about when he would come home and what shape he would be in. Would he be cross with the children? "bearish," critical, or just mellow? She loved Al and wanted to respect him. Barbara was committed to her marriage; for her, marriage was for life—divorce simply wasn't an option.

Over time, Barbara focused more and more on Al's drinking, obsessed more and more with his behavior, protected him and his behavior more and more in order that friends and neighbors wouldn't find out their shameful secret.

Miraculously—after about ten years—Al suddenly stopped drinking. This could only have come from God, thought Barbara, since the suddenness of it was not of this world; it had to be the work of the Holy Spirit! Her prayers were answered. Yet, even though Al did stop drinking, his emotional distance and verbal sharpness did not cease. Al was caught in his compulsion of fixation; he couldn't change his emotional behavior even though he had stopped drinking. He remained emotionally unreliable for Barb. Her thoughts and worries remained focused on Al most of the time. She noticed that her energy level was dropping, even normal things around the house were slipping. Barbara was becoming increasingly and negatively affected on all levels.

One day, Barbara got a call from one of Al's coworkers; he had had a heart attack. She rushed to the hospital to find her husband struggling for his life. Al did survive; he even became a model cardiac rehab patient. Al seemed to find a new addiction—his health (or lack of it). Al became a "professional patient." His whole being was consumed with his sickness. He developed other sicknesses, all of which added yet another layer of worry onto Barbara's already weary mind and heart. Al was a complainer, there seemed nothing that escaped his criticism. With his deteriorating health condition, there was certainly lots to complain about. Naturally, Barbara was the target for most of this complaining. Yet she felt it was her duty to be there for him, to satisfy his every desire, to listen and empathize with his every whim, and to cater to his smallest request. Barbara had lost herself to the unhealthy way her husband was dealing with his sickness.

We are called by God to give service. This applies to our family, and in particular to our spouse. Yet God never calls us to dishonor ourselves in honoring another or to reject our own integrity in support of another's; God never asks us to lose control of ourselves in our attempts to help. Codependency leads us to lose our poise, our spiritual maturity, our graciousness. Most of all, codependency pushes us out of our gifts and into our compulsions; this is separation even from God.

3. The Spiritual Level of Commitment

Love is patient; love is kind; love is not envious or boastful or arrogant or rude. It does not insist on its own way; it is not irritable or resentful; it does not rejoice in wrongdoing, but rejoices in the truth. It bears all things, believes all things, hopes all things, endures all things.

1 CORINTHIANS 13:4-7

Blessed Uniqueness

As the couple condition of *commitment* emerges in the relationship, it facilitates a birth of "blessed uniqueness." Blessed uniqueness is the spiritual relationship condition created in a marriage when each partner acts out of his/her own giftedness in all six personality functions, which allows for a fuller flowering of spiritual distinctiveness and color in the marriage.

The predominant culture widely sees marriage as a legal contract between two people forming a businesslike arrangement of mutual convenience. Such a view diminishes—even discounts—the sacredness that is part of the fabric of the union. Successful seasoned and seasoning marriages have somehow, in their own unique and varied ways, captured the blessing of marriage, and found methods—spoken or unspoken—to celebrate the light and life which this blessing brings to the relationship. Grasping this gift lifts and ennobles any marriage by making us realize that we need to honor it and ourselves throughout the process.

Even on a human level, this "we are blessed" characteristic of a successful seasoned and seasoning relationship is exhibited by an attitude on behalf of both spouses that "this marriage is unique." They genuinely harbor the sense, sometimes communicated while at other times simply understood internally, that this marriage is unlike any other. Seasoned and seasoning partners ultimately can arrive at the heartfelt understanding that not only is this marriage unique, but it is uniquely what I need in a marriage.

Such blessed uniqueness leads us to spiritually embrace everything about our marriage relationship and our spouse. We're not selective about which parts of our marriage and our spouse we will embrace and which parts we won't. We are called to embrace it all. There is no room for denial, rationalization, projection, displacements, or games! For *commitment* to grow into blessed uniqueness, we need to put all of our selves on the line—we cannot hold anything back. Our lot is completely and unequivocally cast with that of our spouse in relationship with God. If we cannot do this, then we are in some way denying the blessed uniqueness that resides in our spouse. This is not only a breach of *commitment,* it's a violation of respect.

The predominant cultural mentality of individualism mitigates against this blessed uniqueness. If my attention is focused, even captured, more on myself than on my spouse, I cannot see the distinctive truth, beauty, and goodness of him or her. If I am acting more on my own behalf than on the behalf of my spouse and our relationship, my perception won't penetrate deeply enough into my spouse's gifts, and I can't truly appreciate his/her uniqueness. If I'm committed only to my self-interest, then I'm the only one who genuinely "counts" in my life. The sin against *commitment* is a breach of love.

Marriage is the most meaningful display of "total belonging" found today. Spouses belong to each other. Spouses are not simply living *with* one another, they are living *as* each other and *for* each other. A facet of blessed uniqueness is fidelity. Fidelity goes far beyond being sexually, emotionally, financially, and socially faithful; it has to do with finding genuine and complete joy in your spouse. This joy cannot be experienced if you are sharing yourself with someone or something else along with your spouse. Such nonexclusion violates fidelity. Fidelity means continuously delighting in one another, without diversion, without exception, full-time, for a lifetime.

CHAPTER EIGHT

Loving for a Lifetime: Using the Six "Essentials" for Marriage Happiness

In the previous pages, we have taken an information-packed and introspective journey into our selves and our marriage relationship. We have studied a new model to help marriages become healthy, happy, and holy on three levels:

1. The individual level: Marriages become most *healthy* when the relationship is seen as an incubator for each spouse to "try out," express, and become strong in his/her unique, God-given gifts.
2. The couple level: Marriages mature to become most *happy* when:
   - each spouse clearly acknowledges and helps the other express his or her unique gifts
   - each partner commits to the six essential competencies of married life
3. The spiritual level: Marriages become most *holy* when the couple embraces God by dedicating the bond they share to God's care.

These three levels are obviously not discrete, distinct, or separate entities—all three work together. When they do work together, the marriage grows like a tree that is given sufficient space, good soil, light, air, warmth, and water. When all the "essentials" needed are in place, the tree of your marriage will bear very good and joyous fruit! When any of these levels is absent or anemic, it will not grow strong—you and your spouse will not be happy!

Let's take the information and the insights you've gained so far and investigate them further by applying them to your particular marriage. Some of the following personal insight extenders are designed to be completed on your own; others can be completed together with your spouse. They can all serve as helpful catalysts in your efforts to advance all six marriage essentials.

Insight One: My Gifts, Shadows, and Compulsions

DIRECTIONS: In the space provided, write your own gifts, shadows, and compulsions in each of the six essentials of a happy, healthy, and holy marriage. Write your gifts in capital letters, so as very boldly to honor the unique powers or energies that God has invested specially in you.

	Compulsion	Gift	Shadow
Togetherness	_____	_____	_____
Respect	_____	_____	_____
Communication	_____	_____	_____
Intimacy	_____	_____	_____
Trust	_____	_____	_____
Commitment	_____	_____	_____

This is your spiritual personality; it is part of God's special fingerprint on you. These gifts are for your spouse as much as they are for you; you may want to discuss these with him or her.

Insight Two: My Life Partner's Gifts, Shadows, and Compulsions

DIRECTIONS: *In the spaces provided, write your spouse's gifts, shadows, and compulsions in each of the six essentials of a happy, healthy, and holy marriage. Write these gifts in capital letters, so as very boldly to honor the unique powers or energies that God has invested specially in him or her.*

	Compulsion	Gift	Shadow
Togetherness			
Respect			
Communication			
Intimacy			
Trust			
Commitment			

This is the spiritual personality of your spouse; it is part of God's special fingerprint on him or her. These gifts are for you as much as they are for your spouse—act accordingly! In our marriage, we are called to:

1. *Honor and cherish our spouse's gifts.*
2. *Learn from his or her shadows.*
3. *Accept the uniqueness of his or her compulsions.*
4. *Forgive always!*

Insight Three:
How My *Gifts* Function in Our Marriage

DIRECTIONS: Write your personal gifts in the spaces provided. Under each gift, write a short statement describing how you see your gift working in your marriage.

1. *My togetherness gift is* _____.
This love-power makes our marriage better by:

2. *My respect gift is* _____.
This love-power makes our marriage better by:

3. *My communication gift is* _____.
This love-power makes our marriage better by:

4. *My intimacy gift is* _____.
This love-power makes our marriage better by:

5. *My trust gift is* _____.
This love-power makes our marriage better by:

6. *My commitment gift is* _____.
This love-power makes our marriage better by:

Insight Four:
How My *Shadows* Function in Our Marriage

DIRECTIONS: *Write the shadows of your personal gifts in the spaces provided. Under each shadow, write a short statement describing how this shadow may function to erode your marriage, however slightly.*

1. The shadow of my togetherness gift is _____.
This shadow may work to erode our marriage by:

2. The shadow of my respect gift is _____.
This shadow may work to erode our marriage by:

3. The shadow of my communication gift is _____.
This shadow may work to erode our marriage by:

4 The shadow of my intimacy gift is _____.
This shadow may work to erode our marriage by:

5. The shadow of my trust gift is _____.
This shadow may work to erode our marriage by:

6. The shadow of my commitment gift is _____.
This shadow may work to erode our marriage by:

Insight Five:
How My *Compulsions* Function in Our Marriage

DIRECTIONS: *Write the compulsions of your personal gifts in the spaces provided. Under each compulsion, write a short statement describing how this compulsion may function to evaporate the life from your marriage, however slightly.*

1. *The compulsion of my togetherness gift is* _____.
This compulsion may work to evaporate the life from our marriage by:

2. *The compulsion of my respect gift is* _____.
This compulsion may work to evaporate the life from our marriage by:

3. *The compulsion of my communication gift is* _____.
This compulsion may work to evaporate the life from our marriage by:

4. *The compulsion of my intimacy gift is* _____.
This compulsion may work to evaporate the life from our marriage by:

5. *The compulsion of my trust gift is* _____.
This compulsion may work to evaporate the life from our marriage by:

6. *The compulsion of my commitment gift is* _____.
This compulsion may work to evaporate the life from our marriage by:

Insight Six:
Questions for Discussion

1. How do you help your spouse express his/her gifts in the marriage?

2. How, specifically, would you like to improve in the area of helping your spouse?

3. How does your spouse help you express your gifts in the marriage?

4. How, specifically, would you like your spouse to improve in the area of helping you express your gifts?

5. What are your three chief goals for your marriage now?

Individual Gifts, Shadows, and Compulsions

TOGETHERNESS:

Compulsion	Gift	Shadow
1. Dependency	God-reliant	Doubt
2. Self-abasement	Humility	Self-centeredness
3. Aloofness	Acceptance	Dissension
4. Legalism	Mercy	Neglect
5. Presumption	Hope	Despair

RESPECT:

Compulsion	Gift	Shadow
6. Illusion	Vision	Blindness
7. Recklessness	Humor	Lamentation
8. Appeasement	Peace	Contention
9. Self-forfeiture	Adaptability	Rigidity
10. Bluntness	Simplicity	Complexity

COMMUNICATION:

Compulsion	Gift	Shadow
11. Overzealousness	Faith	Disloyalty
12. Perfectionism	Wisdom	Inadequacy
13. Sentimentality	Love	Fear
14. Parochialism	Wholeness	Fragmentation
15. Servitude	Charity	Judgment

INTIMACY:

Compulsion	Gift	Shadow
16. Hyper-euphoria	Joyfulness	Dejection
17. Reductionism	Trust	Insecurity
18. Pollyannaism	Love-finder	Fault-seeker
19. Ingratiation	Empathy	Obtuseness
20. Submissiveness	Gratitude	Blame

TRUST:

Compulsion	Gift	Shadow
21. Indecision	Harmony	Chaos
22. Unresponsiveness	Patience	Impulsion
23. Brutishness	Strength	Impotence
24. Unreality	Transcendence	Worldliness
25. Self-repression	Self-discipline	Self-indulgence

COMMITMENT:

Compulsion	Gift	Shadow
26. Skepticism	Honesty/truth	Deceit
27. Excitability	Inspiration	Deadened
28. Co-dependency	Kindness	Indifference
29. Fixated	Steadfast	Unreliability
30. Imperiousness	Perseverance	Resignation

The only way you will objectively know your true "premier" gift is to take the HGP3. My research, comparing the selections that people make of their premier gift on their own with their gifts that emerge on the HGP3, tells me that people's selections and those that are identified on the HGP3 are quite different. There seems to be a tendency for us to select the gifts that seem most socially acceptable, common, or redeemable. We have all these gifts, yet only one is our lead or primary gift. If you want the most accurate appraisal of your true premier gifts, you do need to take the HGP3.[10]

---

[10] See note 2 on page 15.

Notes

Definitions of Shadows and Compulsions

1. *Togetherness:*

a. God-Reliance

shadow: *Doubt* (faithless, dubious, uncertain, incredulous).

compulsion: *Dependency* (taking beliefs from others rather than from self; subordination of spirit to desires of others).

b. Humility

shadow: *Self-centeredness* (conceit, complacency, exaggerated self-confidence).

compulsion: *Self-abasement* (excessive sense of inferiority, guilt, or shame).

c. Acceptance

shadow: *Dissension* (discord, disagreement, clash, working at cross-purposes).

compulsion: *Aloofness* (distancing oneself from situations, persons, and relationships; harboring reserved and cool demeanor).

d. Mercy

shadow: *Indifference* (lack of active interest, detached).

compulsion: *Legalism* (imposing overly strict adherence to rules, laws, and regulations).

e. Hope

shadow: *Despair* (dejection, depression, oppressive emotional weight).

compulsion: *Presumption* (taking "things" for granted).

2. *Respect:*

a. Vision

shadow: *Blindness* (limited perception, dim-sighted, groping in the dark).

compulsion: *Illusion* (engaging in images that are unrealistic).

b. Humor

shadow: *Lamentation* (complain without cause, whine, moan, grumble).

compulsion: *Recklessness* (distorted or irresponsible view of a situation; a thoughtless, foolhardy, rash, inconsiderate outlook).

c. Peace

shadow: *Contention* (oppose, contest, debate, duel, controversy).

compulsion: *Appeasement* (placate, atone, mollify, pacify, soothe to gain goodwill).

d. Adaptability

shadow: *Rigidity* (tight, forceful, overly strict or harsh).

compulsion: *Self-forfeiture* (giving away one's integrity to outside force or person).

e. Simplicity

shadow: *Complexity* (complicated, entangled, disturbing, distorted).

compulsion: *Bluntness* (insensitive, rough, rude, finding it easy to "label").

3. Communication:

a. Faith

shadow: *Disloyalty* (disobedient, rebelling, uncompliant).
compulsion: *Overzealousness* (mind becomes obsessed with one's mission; thinking becomes myopic and self-absorbed).

b. Wisdom

shadow: *Inadequacy* (persistent feelings of inferiority).
compulsion: *Perfectionism* (making unrealistic demands on self and/or others).

c. Love

shadow: *Fear* (alienation, separation, hatred).
compulsion: *Sentimentality* (substituting feeling for thought).

d. Wholeness

shadow: *Fragmentation* (broken, disconnected, off-balance, collapsed).
compulsion: *Parochialism* (thinking becomes narrow, limited, and provincial; shallow, uninteresting, and dull).

e. Charity

shadow: *Judgment* (projecting critical opinion upon another in a repetitive manner; condemnation).
compulsion: *Servitude* (blind service, robot-like thinking, cognitive/mental submission).

4. Intimacy:

a. Joy

shadow: *Rejection* (dispirited, cheerless, dreary).
compulsion: *Hyper-euphoria* (emotional "high" beyond appropriate limits).

b. Trust

shadow: *Insecurity* (shaky, uncertain, not firmly fastened or fixed).
compulsion: *Reductionism* (accept simple formulas and

elementary solutions to life; narrowness of perspective; abhorrence of change).

c. Love-Finder

shadow: *Fault-finding* (seeing blemishes, defects, or imperfections to an excessive degree).

compulsion: *Pollyannaism* (seeing the world through "rose colored glasses"; compelled to feel only positivism, goodwill, and peace).

d. Empathy

shadow: *Obtuseness* (unfeeling, insensible, unmoved, callous, cold).

compulsion: *Ingratiation* (contorting oneself to gain another's favor or good graces).

e. Gratitude

shadow: *Blaming* (critical, guilt-inducing, lacking praise, condemning).

compulsion: *Submissiveness* (excessive beholding to others for your very presence; abnormal devotion in an obsequiousness manner).

5. *Trust:*

a. Harmony

shadow: *Chaos* (disorder, shambles, confusion, conflict, quarrelsome).

compulsion: *Indecision* (paralyzed by doubt; endless hesitation with deciding "what's right").

b. Patience

shadow: *Impulsion* (spontaneous, impetus, compulsion, sudden, thoughtless decision or reaction).

compulsion: *Unresponsiveness* (listless and sluggish, overvigilance against anything that may disrupt lifestyle).

c. Strength

shadow: *Impotence* (powerlessness, weakness, lacking vigor and/or power).

compulsion: *Brutishness* (impelled to quick, indelicate, and heavy-handed discernment).

d. **Transcendence**

shadow: *Worldliness* (material, secular, shallow, sophisticated).

compulsion: *Unreality* (decisions in the realm of fancy, prone to vague daydreams).

e. **Self-discipline**

shadow: *Self-indulgence* (laziness, idleness, no self-control; pandering to the lowest self urges).

compulsion: *Self-repression* (imposing stricture, rather than offering structure; heavy-handed suppression of normal desires).

6. *Commitment:*

a. **Honesty**

shadow: *Deceit* (untrue, fraudulent, trick, cheat, fake).

compulsion: *Skepticism* (posture of repetitious internal questioning; fearful of gullibility).

b. **Inspiration**

shadow: *Deadened* (lifeless, no vigor, lack of spirit).

compulsion: *Excitability* (frenetic and sometimes desperate need for stimulation).

c. **Kindness**

shadow: *Neglect* (giving little or no attention/respect; to disregard).

compulsion: *Codependency* (giving entire self in service to another's dependency).

d. **Steadfastness**

shadow: *Unreliability* (uncertain, undependable, irresponsible).

compulsion: *Fixation* (compelled to keep things exactly as they are or once were).

e. **Perseverance**

shadow: *Resignation* (surrender, terminate, "throw in the towel," withdraw).

compulsion: *Perilousness* (endangering oneself or others unnecessarily).